# cook
## with Stanley

written by Eunice Power

# acknowledgments

This was a team effort so sincere thanks go to Eunice for her passion for this project (and to her family for their patience as we took over her house!); to Christopher, Anike, Ava and Ted Kelly for allowing us to take over their beautiful house and garden (and for modelling!); to Tim and Fiona Yorke for letting us photograph their stunning organic vegetable and herb gardens; to Joan Power for letting us photograph her Stanley and her lovely gardens; to Pat Fleming for his trawlers photograph; to Paul Flynn, Gert Maes and Tim Rooney for their delicious recipes.

I believe that everyone should enjoy good food. My approach to cooking is to keep things simple and seasonal. How, and what we cook varies as our lives and families grow. This cookbook is designed for everyday cooking and caters for all ages and stages of family life. The recipes have been chosen to suit the wonderful cooking qualities of the Stanley range cooker from slow-cooking, roasting and baking right through to stir-frying and grilling.

I grew up with a Stanley range cooker at the heart of our kitchen, so to me Stanley is forever linked with a busy kitchen, full of the usual comings and goings, delicious aromas emanating from the oven whilst football gear is speedily dried on the oven lids!

I have included many recipes for healthy family meals, and also recipes for special occasions and celebrations. A love of good food begins during childhood and this book has lots of recipes that children can enjoy both cooking and eating.

For really healthy, delicious food, it's essential to source the best quality ingredients, preferably locally grown, better still organic and additive free. We are what we eat, so get to know your suppliers and enjoy sourcing and cooking the wonderful food that we produce here in Ireland.

Most important of all take the time to enjoy eating the lovely dishes you have created.

*Eunice Power.*

Eunice Power is a mother of three little boys whose busy life revolves around cooking. Eunice studied Hotel Management in Shannon College of Hotel management and followed up with practical training in Switzerland. Passionate about food, Eunice opened her restaurant in Powersfield House in Dungarvan, Co. Waterford in 2001 where her food was described by John & Sally McKenna's, Bridgestone Guide, as "gee-whizz food from a cook with real verve", and was also listed in Georgina Campbell's Jameson Guide and the AA Guide (where it received the highest rating of 5 Diamonds). Her cooking has been widely praised . As well as running the lovely Powersfield House guest house in Dungarvan, Eunice teaches cooking at the Tannery Cookery school in Dungarvan and runs a very successful outside catering business.

# welcome...

...to the Stanley family, one that stretches back through generations to when the first range cooker was made in Waterford in 1934.

Nothing makes a statement like a Stanley range cooker in your home. Evoking golden childhood memories of a deliciously warm kitchen when casseroles bubbled in the lower oven and the smell of fresh bread wafted throughout the house, it brings so much more to a home than the practical functions of hot water, heating and cooking. However people cooking on today's Stanley are just as likely to be whipping up stir fries and flash-grilling kebabs as turning out the mouthwatering, juicy roasts that the Stanley is famed for.

A new breed of Stanley has also emerged that combines the best features of our traditional cast iron ranges with the flexibility and flair to suit the way you live today. The Stanley Supreme unites the elegant style and timeless qualities you'd expect from our range cookers with state of the art specifications, and it can be fitted directly into your kitchen, without flues or fuss. Available in dual fuel or all electric models, the Supreme offers advanced cooking functions including 2 fan ovens and a superb ceramic grill packaged in a range cooker that retains the Stanley character which brings warmth to any kitchen.

Cooks love their Stanleys! All our range cookers are perfect for baking, ideal for healthy stir-frying or grilling, and wonderful for slow-cooking casseroles and roasts.

To help you get to know your Stanley, we have produced this cookbook containing many recipes which are ideally suited to the exceptional qualities of the Stanley range cooker. Our range cookers belong right at the heart of every home and this is a cookbook for healthy, stylish, everyday family cooking. We hope it marks the beginning of many happy years of cooking on your Stanley!

**From everyone here at Stanley.**

# contents

# breakfast and brunch

apple muesli, recipe page 13

smoothies, recipe page 14

# apple muesli

A favourite as a porridge alternative and perfect for anyone on a dairy-free diet. Ideally choose a sugar and additive free apple juice (an important consideration when catering for small children). You will most probably find a similar type of juice at your local farmer's market. This muesli will last up to a week in your fridge.

Peel and core apples. Slice apples thinly, place in saucepan with sugar, cinnamon and 2 cups of water. Cook to pureé consistency. In a bowl add the apple juice to the oatmeal and stir. Add pureéd apples to mixture. Allow to cool and refrigerate over night. Serve with natural yoghurt and a sprinkling of granola. A wonderfully balanced start to your day.

3 cups organic oatmeal
2 tablespoons sugar
3 cups apple juice
4 cooking apples
1 cinnamon stick
½ cup water
sprinkling of granola

**serves 6**

# granola

This deliciously crunchy granola is as versatile as you want it to be. Keep it interesting by substituting a cup of porridge with sunflower, sesame, linseed or pumpkin seeds or by substituting the raisins for other dried fruits such as chopped apricots or dates.

Preheat the oven to 160°C. Toss the dry ingredients (but not the raisins) together. Add the oil and honey. Toss again to coat thoroughly. Spread the mixture on greaseproof paper in your largest roasting tin and bake until golden, turning every 10 minutes so it browns evenly. When done, after about 30 minutes add the raisins and let cool. It will lose its stickiness and become crunchy. Serve with Greek yoghurt and bananas.

6 cups organic porridge oats
1 cup chopped nuts
1 cup wheat germ
1 teaspoon grated nutmeg
1 tablespoon ground cinnamon
Pinch of salt
1 cup raisins
½ cup sunflower oil
¾ cup honey

**serves 10**

# perfect porridge in three minutes

Oats provide slow-energy release with a low glycaemic index which makes them a particularly good start to the day. For a change, serve with stewed fruits such as rhubarb or apple.

In a saucepan stir oat flakes into water or milk. Bring to the boil and cook briskly for 3 minutes. Flavour as desired and serve.

1 cup of organic oat flakes
2½ cups of cold water or milk

**serves 2**

# smoothies

The following are some smoothie suggestions. All are quite versatile using fruit in season and are a super way of fooling children into eating fruit. For small babies, mix with baby rice (for a really nutritious breakfast or lunch) or with breakfast cereals (a great way to cut down on dairy intake for dietary reasons).

## banana

1 ripe banana
1 teaspoon honey
¾ cup of milk
½ teaspoon vanilla essence
¼ cup of yoghurt
Juice of 2 oranges

**serves 1**

Purée the banana, milk, yoghurt, orange juice and honey in a blender, then add enough vanilla to give it a good flavour.

## strawberry

6oz strawberries
1 banana
Juice of two oranges

**serves 1**

Remove green stem from strawberries. Purée all ingredients together.

## pear

1 cup pear juice*
1 ripe pear*
2 drops almond essence
1 cup yoghurt

**serves 1**

Purée everything until smooth then pour over ice.

*Pears tinned in their own juice may be used. Tinned fruit in its juice (with no sugar added) is a brilliant substitute for fresh fruit in winter. Purée everything until smooth then pour over ice.

# rhubarb and strawberries in rosewater syrup

**Served with greek yoghurt this is a sumptuous breakfast treat. Try it as a dessert with some vanilla ice-cream.**

**rosewater syrup**
1 pint/600ml water
1 lb/900g sugar
1 dessert spoon rose water
(available at your local chemist)

Dissolve the sugar in the water over a gentle heat and boil for three minutes. Remove from heat.
Add the rosewater and allow to cool.

**stewed rhubarb
& strawberries**
1lb/450g (eight stalks)
of pink rhubarb
1 punnet of strawberries

Cut the rhubarb into 22cm/1inch pieces and place in a stainless steel saucepan with the rosewater syrup. Cover and bring to the boil for 1 minute. Remove from heat immediately and allow to cool in the saucepan. Add sliced strawberries to the cooled cooked rhubarb and serve.

brown bread, recipe page 96

bruschetta with tomato, mushrooms and goat's cheese, recipe opposite page

# french toast with apple and cinnamon butter and clonakilty black pudding

A marvellous contrast of colours and flavours make this a fantastic brunch dish! The solid top of the Stanley is perfect for French toast, giving it an even golden finish.

Paul Flynn's recipe – The Tannery, Dungarvan.

### apple and cinnamon butter

Melt the butter until foaming. Add the cinnamon, cook for one minute and throw in the apples. Cook over a medium heat for five to eight minutes. Add the cider, then cook for another 15 minutes. Finally add the sugar until you get a nice sweet/sour balance. Purée with a hand blender.
It will be quite runny and a nice cinnamon colour. Allow to cool. This can be made in advance and stored in your fridge for up to two weeks or in your freezer for up to a month. This recipe is also a superb accompaniment to cheer up pork chops!

### french toast

Whisk eggs, salt and milk together in a basin. Melt butter in frying pan. Dip slices of bread into the egg mixture and place on heated pan. Cook on each side until golden brown. Repeat with all bread.

### clonakilty black pudding

Cut pudding into 18 x 1 inch slices (allowing 3 slices per portion). Melt knob of butter on heated pan, when sizzling add pudding and cook on each side. Remove from heat.

To assemble the dish, spread apple and cinnamon butter on each slice of french toast and crumble 3 slices of cooked black pudding on top. Before serving each portion, put in hot oven for 5 minutes. Serve piping hot.

**apple and cinnamon butter**
7oz/200g butter
2lb/900g cooking apples peeled, cored and diced
2 tablespoons ground cinnamon
4 fl oz/120ml dry cider
Demerara sugar to taste

**french toast**
3 large eggs
6 slices of white bread
6 fl oz/175ml milk
pinch of salt
2oz/50g butter

**clonakilty black pudding**
1 large clonakilty black pudding

**serves 6**

# bruschetta with tomato, mushrooms and goat's cheese

A delicious hot breakfast, made even better with the addition of some home-made chutney (see page 122) served on the side.

Turn grill on to full power. Toast the bread on both sides until crisp and golden. Slice mushrooms, quarter tomatoes. Melt butter in frying pan until sizzling. Add mushrooms and tomatoes. Season with salt and freshly ground black pepper and fry for 4–5 minutes, stirring occasionally. Place mushroom and tomato mixture on each slice of bread and top with goat's cheese. Place under grill until goat's cheese begins to melt and serve.

4 thickly cut slices of vienna loaf
4 slices goat's cheese
½ lb/225g tomatoes
½ lb/225g mushrooms
Butter for frying
Salt and freshly ground black pepper

**serves 4**

# smoked salmon with scrambled egg and chives

**Creamy scrambled eggs with succulent smoked salmon – can you think of a better start to your day?**

8 free-range eggs
2 tablespoons milk or cream
Salt and freshly ground black pepper
1 tablespoon chopped chives
2oz/50g butter
8 slices of smoked salmon

**serves 4**

Line four teacups with sliced smoked salmon. Break eggs into a bowl, add milk, season with salt and pepper and mix with a whisk. Melt 1oz/25g butter in a thick-bottomed pan, add the eggs and cook over a gentle heat stirring continuously until eggs are lightly cooked. Remove from heat, correct the seasoning, stir in the chives and remaining 1oz/25g butter. (A tablespoon of cream may be added) Spoon the scrambled egg into the smoked salmon lined cups. Turn the cups onto a slice of buttered toast and unmould the smoked salmon and scrambled eggs. Serve with a lemon wedge – very impressive!

# oat pancakes with summer berries

**The combination of oats, milk, eggs and fruit makes this a nutritious start to the day.**

125g plain flour
1tsp baking powder
½ tsp salt
25g caster sugar
75g porridge oats
2 large eggs
250ml whole milk
Vegetable oil & butter to cook

300g fresh berries
Juice of 1 orange
Sugar to taste

**serves 4**

Sift the flour, baking powder and salt in a large bowl. Stir in the oats and sugar. In a separate bowl lightly whisk together the milk and eggs. Pour the milk mixture into the egg mixture and using a fork beat until you have a smooth batter. Let the batter stand for a few minutes. Heat a griddle pan or large heavy based non stick frying pan over a medium heat. Add a drop of oil and knob of butter to the pan. When the butter has melted add a dessertspoon of the batter to the pan. Cook for 2–3 minutes until bubbles start to break through on surface, then turn it over and cook until both sides are golden brown and the pancake has risen to about 1cm thick. Transfer to a warm oven until the remaining pancakes are cooked.

Place the fresh berries in a small saucepan, add the orange juice and gently heat. Add sugar to desired taste.

soups and canapés

smoked haddock chowder with sweetcorn and sweet potato, recipe page 26

spicy carrot and tomato soup, recipe opposite page // pea and mint soup with parmesan, recipe page 24 // minestrone soup, recipe page 25

# spicy carrot and roasted tomato soup

The roasting of juicy vine tomatoes with herbs combines beautifully with the sweetness of the spicy carrots.

Preheat the oven to 150°C. Place tomatoes in a roasting dish, trickle over the olive oil, vinegar, herbs and honey, sprinkle with salt and pepper, pierce tomatoes with garlic slivers bake for 35/40 minutes until softened. Melt the butter, add the onions and sweat for a few minutes. Add the garlic, carrots, saffron, cumin, coriander, sherry and ¾ teaspoon of salt, cover with dampened double sided greaseproof paper, put lid on saucepan and cook gently for 20 minutes, until the carrots are thoroughly impregnated with butter and spice. Pour boiling stock over the mixture and simmer for about 30 minutes until the carrots are soft. Add to roasted tomatoes and liquidise. Reheat and serve in warmed bowls.

**roasted tomatoes**

**soup**

**serves 6**

# french onion soup

This is a heart-warming classic soup on a cold winter's day.

Melt the butter in a heavy based saucepan on the simmering plate, add the onions and cook gently for about 30 minutes stirring occasionally until golden brown. Be careful not to let the onions burn, as they will have a bitter taste. Gradually add the stock and the Worcestershire sauce, season, cover with a lid and simmer for about 40 minutes. Toast the bread, divide cheese between the four slices. Place on a baking tray and put in main oven until the cheese has melted (about 5 minutes). Place a slice of bread in each soup bowl and pour over the soup. Serve immediately.

**serves 4**

# pea & mint soup with parmesan

**This vibrant green soup is very quick and easy to prepare. The mint cuts through the sweetness of the peas, lifting and freshening the soup's flavour.**

In a large pan, sauté the onion and garlic gently in the oil and butter until soft. Add two thirds of the peas, mint and stock. Cover, bring to the boil and simmer for 5 minutes. Whizz the soup in a food processor until smooth. Return to the pan and add the remaining stock and peas. Season and cook gently on simmering ring for five minutes. Finely chop the remaining mint and add to the soup. Divide the Parmesan into 6 equal portions and place a mound in six soup bowls. Pour the soup around the mounds, drizzle with olive oil and serve.

1 large red onion
1 garlic clove peeled and sliced
1 tablespoon extra-virgin olive oil, plus a little for serving
1oz/25g butter
800g/1¾ lbs. frozen peas
1 bunch of fresh mint leaves, chopped
1 litre/1¾ pints home made vegetable stock
Salt and freshly ground black pepper
3oz/75g freshly grated parmesan

**serves 6**

# instant spring vegetable soup

**Quick, easy and fresh – the best kind of soup to make! A great way of using up leftovers and the perfect snack for hungry children (and adults!) when they arrive in the door.**

Place the vegetables in the liquidiser and sprinkle over the stock cube. Allow the boiled water to cool for 2 minutes then pour into the liquidiser to cover the vegetables. Blend at minimum speed for 2–4 minutes, then season to taste with salt and freshly ground black pepper. Serve immediately.

*If you have home-made stock use instead of the stock cube.

2 medium potatoes, cooked
1 carrot cleaned, chopped and cooked
1 leek, white and light green part only, cleaned cut into 1 inch/2cm pieces and cooked
1 fresh tomato
1 stock cube, either vegetable, beef or chicken
(I find the organic stock cubes "Kallo" excellent)
600g/1 pint of freshly boiled water*
Salt and freshly milled pepper

**serves 4**

# minestrone soup

This robust soup is a meal in itself. Don't be put off by all the ingredients and chopping, your efforts will be justly rewarded.

In a large saucepan heat the oil and butter. Cook the onion, until soft but not browned. Add the diced carrots and cook for 2–3 minutes, stirring once or twice, repeat the procedure using the celery, courgette, green beans and cabbage. Cook for about 6 minutes, giving the pot an occasional stir.

Add the broth and the tomatoes in their juice, cover and cook at a slow simmer for 1 hour. Stir the soup occasionally, the soup should be thick, but add a cup of water if becoming too thick. Add the tinned beans and spaghetti 20 minutes before serving. To serve ladle the thick soupy mixture into bowls and top generously with grated parmesan.

6 tablespoons of golden olive oil
2oz/50g butter
4 medium onions finely sliced
4 carrots diced
2 sticks of celery, diced
10oz/250g spaghetti broken into small pieces
2 courgettes diced
3½oz/100g green beans
2 handfuls of finely sliced cabbage
2½ pints/1½ litres beef stock (3 beef stock cubes dissolved in 1½ litres boiling water)
14oz/400g tin chopped tomatoes
14oz/400g tin white beans (e.g cannellini) rinsed and drained
Freshly grated parmesan cheese to serve

**serves 6**

# nettle soup

The nearest you will get to a free dinner! Nettle soup should be made in May when the nettles are young and tender. Nettles were traditionally used in cooking for medicinal purposes as they are high in iron. It goes without saying …wear gloves when handling nettles!

Heat the butter and oil in a heavy based pan until foaming, add the onion, leek and potato, cover with greaseproof paper and simmer gently for 10 minutes until softened but not coloured. Add the stock and bring to the boil, simmer until vegetables are cooked. Add the nettles and simmer for 2/3 minutes. Liquidise the soup, return to saucepan, stir in crème fraîche and season to taste. Serve hot.

1oz/25g butter
1 tablespoon sunflower oil
1 large onion chopped
2 leeks washed and chopped
3 medium potatoes peeled and diced
1½ pint/900ml home-made chicken stock
2 bunches of nettles
salt and freshly ground pepper
¼ pint/150ml crème fraîche

**serves 6**

# smoked haddock chowder
# with sweetcorn & sweet potato

**This visually stunning soup is bursting with colour and flavour. A handful of torn basil adds an unusually aromatic flavour.**

Cut the haddock into 5 pieces. Place in a shallow pan and cover with pint/600ml water add the bay leaf, parsley and lemon. Bring to a simmer and cook for 5 minutes. Remove the haddock, break it up using a fork and set aside. Strain the stock and set aside. Melt the butter in a large pan over a medium heat; add the onion and sweet potato and cook for 5 minutes, stirring until just starting to soften around the edges. Add the reserved fish stock; boil for 10-15 minutes until the sweet potatoes are tender. Add the milk, bring to just a simmer then add the flaked haddock and sweetcorn. Cook at a bare simmer for a minute or two. Stir in the cream and basil. Season with salt and pepper to taste.

1lb/500g of smoked haddock
fillets, skin removed
1 bay leaf
A few stalks of parsley
1 slice of lemon
2oz/50g butter
1 onion finely chopped
2 orange fleshed sweet
potatoes peeled and cubed
1 pint/600ml milk
5oz/150g tinned sweet corn
2-3 tablespoons of single
cream
1 handful of fresh basil, torn
into pieces

**serves 4**

# tomato and basil soup

**This soup is an all time family favourite. If you are not a basil fan then mint, coriander, rosemary or indeed the finely grated zest of an orange can be substituted for the basil. Traditionally a summertime soup using up the glut of fresh tomatoes but in wintertime tinned tomatoes are a good alternative.**

Gently heat the olive oil and add the onions and potatoes. Cover and cook until soft but not coloured. Add the tomatoes, garlic, stock and sugar and bring to the boil. Simmer gently for 25 minutes. Add the basil then liquidise the soup, season and bring back to the boil for 1 or 2 minutes. Serve with a blob of cream and some torn basil leaves. Alternatively drizzle with some basil pesto.

1½ tablespoons olive oil
1½lbs/700g ripe tomatoes or
two 14oz/400g tins of tinned
tomatoes
1 medium onion chopped
finely
1 clove of garlic chopped finely
1 medium potato diced
10fl oz/275ml stock, vegetable
or chicken
½ dessert spoon of sugar
2 teaspoons torn fresh basil
leaves

**serves 6**

# tomato, roast red pepper and goat's cheese soup

**For a different flavour try this…**

Follow the tomato soup recipe adding a roast red pepper skinned with pips removed and 3oz of goat's cheese when liquidising the soup. Serve with a mini crostini with melted goat's cheese… delicious!

langoustines with lime mayonnaise on ice, recipe page 28

# canapés

## asparagus wrapped in Parma ham with Parmesan butter

16 asparagus spears, with ends cut off
16 slices parma ham
2-3 tbsp olive oil
25g/1oz unsalted butter, softened
40g/1 1/2oz freshly grated parmesan
1 tbsp chives, chopped
1/2 tbsp basil, chopped

**serves 4**

For the parmesan butter, beat together the butter, parmesan, chives and basil. Transfer the mixture to parchment paper and roll into a log. Refrigerate.

Blanch the asparagus in a pan of salted boiling water for 2 minutes, then drain and refresh in a bowl of cold water. Remove from the water and dry in a clean towel.

Wrap each asparagus spear in a slice of parma ham and drizzle with olive oil. Season with black pepper. Cook under a hot grill for 5-6 minutes, turning occasionally until the ham is crispy.

Serve with crusty bread and Parmesan butter.

## langoustines with lime mayonnaise on crushed ice

**Delicious succulent langoustines are a memorable beginning to any evening. Remember to leave a dish nearby for shells.**

Allow 5-6 langoustines per person
6 tablespoons of good quality mayonnaise
Juice of one lime
Lime wedges

Remove entrails from langoustines by taking the middle segment or tail shell between thumb and forefinger then twist it and pull. Plunge langoustines into simmering water for 30–40 seconds. Remove and leave to cool naturally. Mix the lime juice with the mayonnaise. To serve arrange the langoustines on a bed of crushed ice, place lime mayonnaise in a bowl in the centre of the dish and scatter lime wedges. Enjoy!

# pitta crisps with dips

**These are easy to make and handy to use with dips. Each of the recipes below makes a generous bowl.**

Cut pitta bread into wedges, toss in some light olive oil, salt, chopped garlic and some thyme, drain off excess oil on kitchen paper then finish off in a hot oven until crispy – be careful not to over do. Store in an airtight container for a few days.

Beware… don't use too much olive oil as the pitta will be soggy, use just enough to coat the pitta wedges.

# hummus

Drain the chickpeas and whiz in a blender or food processor to make a smooth paste. Add the lemon juice, garlic, tahini paste, olive oil, smoked paprika and salt to taste. Blend to a soft creamy texture. Taste and continue to add lemon juice and salt until you are happy with the flavour. Pour into a serving dish.

Serve as a dip with pitta crisps.

**serves 4**

# baba ghanoush

Baba ghanoush is a favourite on mezze tables throughout the Middle East and Lebanon. When you taste it you will know why. This dip can be served with pitta crisps or as an accompaniment to lamb tagine. The sharp flavour of the baba ghanoush offers a wonderful contrast to the aromatic sweet flavour of the tagine. The quantities below are guidelines, as it depends on the size of the aubergine, so taste is the best judge of all.

Heat the oil in a medium frying pan. Add the garlic and sauté for 2 minutes. Add the aubergine and fry for 6–8 minutes, or until soft. Transfer the garlic and aubergine to a food processor. Add the remaining ingredients and blitz to purée. Spoon the baba ghanoush into a bowl.

**serves 4**

smoked chicken, swiss chard and pecan nut tart, recipe page 42

## cocktail sausages with pear chutney

Cocktail sausages appeal to all age groups and are often the first canapés to disappear. This is a very simple way to add a little extra flavour to our popular friends.

Cook the sausages on a baking tray in a hot oven. When cooked, pat the sausages with a piece of kitchen paper to remove excess grease. Put the sausages in an ovenproof dish, add the chutney and stir until all sausages are coated. Re-heat in a hot oven for a few minutes when ready to serve.

2lbs/900g cocktail sausages
1 tablespoons of pear chutney
(see page 122)

## devils on horseback

These little devils are easy to prepare, tasty little treats.

Split prunes and fill with chutney. Roll each prune in half a slice of streaky bacon. Place the little devils on a baking tray and bake in the middle of the oven for 10 minutes or until the bacon is cooked.

Easy entertaining tip…Prepare in advance and store in fridge until needed.

10 streaky bacon rashers,
cut in half and flattened with
a rolling pin.
20 stoned prunes
Pear chutney or whatever fruit
chutney you have in your
cupboard
(see page 122)

**serves 20**

## red pepper aioli

A staple in your fridge during the summer, dressing up a simple salad or a posh ketchup for barbecue burgers!

Using a food processor put the peppers, garlic, egg yolks and salt into the bowl and blitz until paste forms. Trickle oil in slowly until the mixture thickens to mayonnaise. Season with smoked paprika. Delicious served with crudités i.e. carrot batons, celery stalks, florets of broccoli and cauliflower.

Cheat's red pepper aioli
Whizz a roast red pepper, 2 cloves of garlic and 8fl oz/240ml good quality mayonnaise in a food processor and there you have it!

1 roast red pepper, skin
removed
1 - 2 garlic cloves peeled and
chopped
½ teaspoon salt
2 large egg yolks at room
temperature
8 fl oz/240ml golden olive oil
½ teaspoon smoked paprika

Basil is a native plant of India which explains why it does not survive out of doors in our Irish climate. Basil can be grown from seed, and pots of green and purple basil will live happily on your kitchen windowsill. Beware - basil's biggest enemy is white fly which appear as the weather gets warmer, in which case make sure to rinse the leaves before use.

# tiny crostini with onion marmalade and feta cheese

These tasty little canapés can be made larger and served with some tossed leaves as a starter or light lunch. The onion marmalade can be stored in your fridge for a week in a sealed container and is great with steaks, as a pizza topping, or to liven up a pasta dish.

**crostini**
1 baguette
1 tablespoon olive oil
1 peeled clove of garlic
½ quantity onion marmalade
(see page 122)

Preheat the oven to 200°C. Cut the baguette into 1 inch / 2½ cm slices. Brush each side of the baguette slices with olive oil. Place slices of baguette on a baking tray and bake in the middle of the oven for 3 minutes until crisp and golden. Remove from oven and gently rub each crostini with garlic.

Pile onions onto crostini and place a chunk of feta cheese on top. Enjoy!

# vol au vents with mediterranean ratatouille and boilie cheese

Frozen Vol au Vent cases are so handy, always have a supply in the freezer for emergencies! If you can't source Boilie, a wonderful Irish cheese in oil, any soft cheese will work equally well.

12 mini vol au vents
½ quantity of ratatouille
(see page 93)
6 Boilie cheese balls

Bake vol au vents according to instructions on pack. Fill each vol au vent with ratatouille (see page 93) and pop half a ball of Boilie cheese on top. Just before serving reheat in hot oven 180°C for 7–10 minutes and serve.

**serves 4**

Feta cheese is a classic and famous curd cheese whose tradition dates back thousands of years and is still being made by shepherds in the Greek Mountains. It was originally made with unpasturised goat's and sheep's milk but today it is often made with cow's milk. I buy Waterford feta, your deli or farmer's market will stock your local variety.

tiny crostini with onion marmalade and feta cheese, recipe opposite page

starters and light lunches

the perfect green salad with garden herb dressing, recipe page 43

# chicken liver parfait

I adore smooth creamy chicken liver parfait and have been chasing the recipe for years. It is all things to all men, starter, lunch, snack. The flavour and texture is truly decadent.

Place the port, Madeira, brandy and thyme in a pan and simmer until reduced to a couple of tablespoonfuls. Remove and discard the thyme. Chop the chicken livers and warm through in a pan. Sprinkle over the salt, then transfer to a food processor and add the reduced port mixture, shallots and garlic. Process to a coarse purée, then gradually add the eggs and melted butter. Purée again until smooth, then pass through a sieve and spoon into a terrine dish*. Cover tightly with aluminium foil. Place in a roasting tin half filled with warm water and cook in a very low oven 110°C/225F for 90 minutes. When cooked, remove from the roasting tin, cool and refrigerate for 24 hours. To serve, whisk the butter, sunflower oil and pepper together and spread a very thin layer on top of the parfait. Run a hot knife around the edges and turn out on to a board. Spread the flavoured butter over the other sides. When the butter has set wrap in cling film until needed. To serve cut into thin slices, using a hot knife. Serve with toasted or warm crusty bread and a little onion marmalade (see page 119) if you have some in the fridge.

*Use a 2lb loaf tin lined with cling film. This will last a week in the fridge.

4fl oz/100ml ruby port
4fl oz/100ml Madeira
(or medium dry sherry)
2fl oz/50ml brandy
1 sprig of thyme
14oz/400g fresh chicken livers
1 tsp salt
5oz/150g finely sliced shallots
2 garlic cloves, peeled and finely sliced
14oz/400g butter, melted
4 eggs

**to serve**
4½/125g softened butter
1fl oz/25ml truffle oil, or sunflower oil.
½ teaspoon cracked black pepper

**serves 10**

# rillettes of salmon with wholegrain mustard and capers

A classic starter using fresh and smoked salmon and packed with herby flavours.

Mix all the ingredients together. Serve lightly chilled. This is delicious served as a canape on little crostini or as a starter with melba toast and cucumber pickle (see page 117).

8oz/200g poached salmon flaked
6oz/150g smoked salmon (cut into ½ cm dice)
3 teaspoons crème fraîche
1 teaspoon wholegrain mustard
1 teaspoon chopped dill
1 teaspoon chopped chives
1 dessertspoon of chopped capers
salt and pepper
1 pinch cayenne pepper
1 squeeze lemon juice

**serves 4**

# potted crab with ginger and lime

**Serve this delicate starter with melba toast and cucumber pickle (see page 120) on the side.**

250g pack unsalted butter, cut
into cubes
2½ (1in) piece fresh root
ginger, finely grated
3 spring onions, finely sliced
12–13oz/350–375g white and
brown crab meat
Juice of ½ lime
1 lime cut into thin slices

**serves 6**

Clarify the butter by putting it into a small pan and melting it over a low heat without stirring. Bring the butter to the boil and simmer it for 1-2 minutes until a white foam appears on the surface. Carefully skim the foam away with a slotted spoon and discard it. Allow the butter to settle, then carefully pour it into a second pan, leaving the milky sediment behind (discard this sediment). Put 5 tablespoons of the clarified butter to one side. Add the grated root ginger and the sliced spring onions to the clarified butter remaining in the pan and cook them gently for 2-3 minutes until the onions are soft. Leave them to cool, then add them to the crab meat along with the lime juice. Season with salt and freshly ground black pepper and mix well. Spoon the mixture into six 150ml (4 pint) ramekins or pots. Smooth the surface of each and put a lime slice on top. Pour a thin layer of reserved butter over each pot, cover and chill until the butter is set. Remove the pots from the fridge 20 minutes before serving.

# light lunches and salads

## flat cap mushrooms with bacon and goat's cheese

**This recipe comes into its own in August when fields, just like magic, turn white with a crop of luscious mushrooms of all shapes and sizes.**

4 large flat cap field
mushrooms
3 tablespoons olive oil
2oz/50g butter
2oz/50g rindless bacon, finely
chopped
2 large cloves of garlic, peeled
and crushed
4oz/100g breadcrumbs
2 tablespoons chopped basil
2oz/50g goat's cheese,
crumbled
1 tablespoon lemon juice
Toasted pine nuts
Freshly ground salt and pepper

Cut stalks from mushrooms and chop them finely reserving the whole caps. Heat 2 tablespoons oil in a frying pan, add the mushroom caps, rounded side down, and fry for one minute to brown. Transfer to a baking sheet. Melt the butter, add the chopped mushroom stalks, bacon and garlic to the frying pan and fry for 5 minutes, then transfer to a bowl. Add the breadcrumbs, basil, goat's cheese, lemon juice and seasoning and mix well. Divide the stuffing between the mushroom cups. Drizzle the remaining oil over the top and bake at 200°C for 20 minutes until crisp and golden. To serve sprinkle generously with toasted pine nuts and torn basil leaves.

flat cap mushrooms with bacon and goat's cheese, recipe opposite page

# oriental prawn salad

This plum dressing is perfect when used with fresh or frozen prawns and gives an oriental twist to a prawn starter.

Blitz all the dressing ingredients in a food processor. Toss prawns and sliced vegetables in plum dressing and divide into 4 portions and serve on individual plates, sprinkled with sesame seeds.

When fresh prawns are not available I use frozen king prawns defrosted in the fridge overnight. While defrosting add 1 teaspoon of anchovy sauce to the prawns, this improves the flavour.

**plum dressing**
1 spring onion
2 fresh ripe plums
5 tablespoons sunflower oil
2 tablespoons sherry vinegar
2 teaspoons soy sauce
2 teaspoons sundried tomato pesto
1 clove crushed garlic
¼ – ½ teaspoon brown sugar

**prawn salad**
4 spring onions, finely sliced lengthways
4oz/100g sugar snap peas sliced lengthways
8oz/200g peeled prawns
½ shredded iceberg lettuce
4oz/100g cherry tomatoes, halved
1 tablespoon sesame seeds/ sunflower seeds

# salmon fishcakes

These can be prepared beforehand and cooked when you are ready to eat. Serve as a light lunch with a crispy organic leaf salad or as a starter. Use a fish shape cookie cutter to shape fish cakes for children, making them more fun to eat. Enjoy!

Heat the oven to 190°C. Put the fish in a roasting tin and cover with water, and a few lemon slices. Cover with tin foil and cook in the oven for about 10–15 minutes until opaque and starting to flake. When cool enough to handle, take off the skin, remove any bones and flake the fish into large chunks. Mix the fish, potato, parsley and capers together with enough of the egg to bind the mixture. Mix together carefully so as not to break up the fish too much. Season well. Shape into 8–12 patties, depending on how large you want them to be and chill thoroughly. Heat some vegetable oil in a frying pan and heat the fish cakes until golden brown on each side and heated right through.

I serve these with caper mayonnaise. Mix 1 quantity mayonnaise (see page 117) with a tablespoon of chopped capers.

450g/1lb salmon
2 tablespoons freshly chopped parsley
1 quantity mashed potato
2 tablespoons of capers
1 egg, beaten.
Salt and freshly ground black pepper
Vegetable oil, for frying

**makes 8 generous fishcakes**

# thai chicken and peanut salad

**This is a yummy salad. Inspired by Thai flavours, it can be made with everyday store cupboard ingredients.**

10oz/750g/1lb cooked chicken
3oz/70g noodles, broken into small pieces
3 cloves garlic, lightly smashed
1 small bunch coriander
1 tablespoon coriander leaves for garnish
3 ½ oz/85g smooth peanut butter
2 tablespoons light soy sauce
1 tablespoon clear honey
1 teaspoon chilli oil
1 tablespoon rice vinegar
1 teaspoon dry sherry
1 cucumber, peeled, seeded and cut into strips
4 spring onions shredded
1 carrot cut into thin strips
Sweet chilli sauce for drizzling

**serves 4**

Dice the chicken. Pour very hot water over the noodles and soak for 5 minutes. In a food processor, blend the garlic, coriander, peanut butter, soy sauce, honey, chilli oil, vinegar and sherry and blend until smooth. Toss the chicken in the sauce until coated. Divide noodles between four serving plates, top with cucumber strips, carrot strips, spring onion and the chicken. Drizzle with sweet chilli sauce and sprinkle with coriander leaves to serve.

# smoked chicken, swiss chard and pecan nut tart

**A delicious twist on a savoury quiche, the Swiss chard can be substituted with spinach.**

1 smoked chicken breast
12 stems of swiss chard
12 pecan nuts
3 large free range eggs and 1 yolk
¼ pint/125ml cream
¼ pint/125ml milk

**serves 6**

Line a 9½ inch/24cm tin with short crust pastry. Pre heat the oven to 200ºC. Steam the swiss chard until wilted (2/3 minutes). Line the pastry case with greaseproof paper and baking beans. Bake at 200ºC for 8–10 minutes until golden. Reduce the oven temperature to 190ºC. Arrange the slices of smoked chicken breast and Swiss chard on the base of the tart. Beat the milk, cream and egg together and pour over. Scatter the pecan nuts on top. Bake in the oven for 30–35 minutes or until the filling is set. Serve warm with green salad.

# purple sprouting broccoli with lemon mayonnaise

**Purple sprouting broccoli is the first of the summer vegetables. Treat it like asparagus and serve it as a delicious light lunch on its own or as a starter.**

1lb/500g purple sprouting broccoli
½ quantity mayonnaise (see page 117)
Juice of ½ lemon
Tablespoon of chopped parsley

**serves 4**

Rinse the broccoli and steam for a couple of minutes until tender. Combine mayonnaise, parsley and lemon juice. Serve hot broccoli with mayonnaise for dipping.

# winter red cabbage salad

**Delicious served with roast poultry and game or alternatively as a cold salad crumbled with feta or blue cheese. The addition of walnut gives a lovely crunch while the parsley adds a fresh flavour.**

Carefully toast walnut pieces on a low heat in dry pan. Cut cabbage into medium slices, do not use a food processor for this, a sharp knife gives better results. Heat oil. Add onions, garlic and cabbage. Fry for 2–3mins until it wilts. Add walnuts, apple and balsamic vinegar and cook for another few minutes. Season. Mix in parsley. Serve on warmed plates and top with feta cheese.

2oz walnut pieces or roughly chopped pecan nuts
450g/1lb red cabbage
2 teaspoons light oil
4 spring onions trimmed and finely sliced
1 garlic clove peeled and finely chopped
1 large apple sliced/grated
3 teaspoons balsamic vinegar
Salt and pepper
A handful of flat leaved parsley (roughly chopped)
4oz cubed feta cheese

**serves 4**

# the perfect green salad with dressing

In the summer why not try growing your own salad leaves, they don't take up very much space and can be grown very successfully in tubs or window boxes. Rather than picking the whole plant, leaves can be picked from the outside as you need them and the plant will continue to grow. Salad leaves can be grown very successfully from seed or alternatively they can be purchased in garden centres, at your local farmers market or from your local organic vegetable grower.

If you are buying salad, choose the freshest of leaves, organically grown when possible. Wash immediately and store in the fridge. Mix herbs such as flat leaf parsley, basil, coriander and chives with salad leaves for extra flavour.

Salad leaves ought to be treated with the greatest of care. To wash your salad leaves fill the sink with cold water and add a little salt; (the salt helps to detach determined slugs). Drop the leaves in the sink and gently wash, taking care not to damage the leaves. I then dry the leaves in a salad spinner, don't over fill the salad spinner, as the leaves will get bruised. When dressing a salad do so at the very last minute, being careful not to overdress causing the leaves to be heavy and oily.

# salad dressings

The general rule of thumb for salad dressings is 3 parts oil to one part vinegar, salt and freshly milled pepper. I tend to use 2 parts olive oil to 1 part sunflower oil as I find olive oil can be a little heavy on its own. Depending on the end flavour you wish to achieve balsamic vinegar, white wine vinegar, rice vinegar, cider vinegar or lemon juice can be used in your dressing.

# greek salad dressing

2 tablespoons freshly squeezed lemon juice
5 tablespoons extra virgin olive oil
1 tablespoon sunflower oil
Sea salt and freshly milled pepper

Whisk all ingredients together. Serve with green leaves, juicy plum tomatoes, olives and feta cheese.

# honey and mustard dressing

6 tablespoons extra virgin olive oil
2 tablespoons white wine vinegar
1 small clove of garlic crushed
1 teaspoon of grain mustard
2 teaspoons of local runny honey
Sea salt and freshly milled pepper

Whisk all ingredients together.

# garden herb dressing

6 tablespoons extra virgin olive oil
2 tablespoons white wine vinegar
1 small clove of garlic crushed
1 teaspoon of finely chopped garden herbs, choose from parsley, rosemary, thyme or mint
Sea salt and freshly milled pepper

Whisk all ingredients together.

*Interesting additions to salads:*

*Try adding, toasted nuts, walnuts, pinenuts, olives, parmesan shavings, crispy croutons, apple slices, crumbled or cubed cheese to your green salads to make them even more interesting.*

meat

Sirloin steak with onion marmalade and potato cakes, recipe page 50

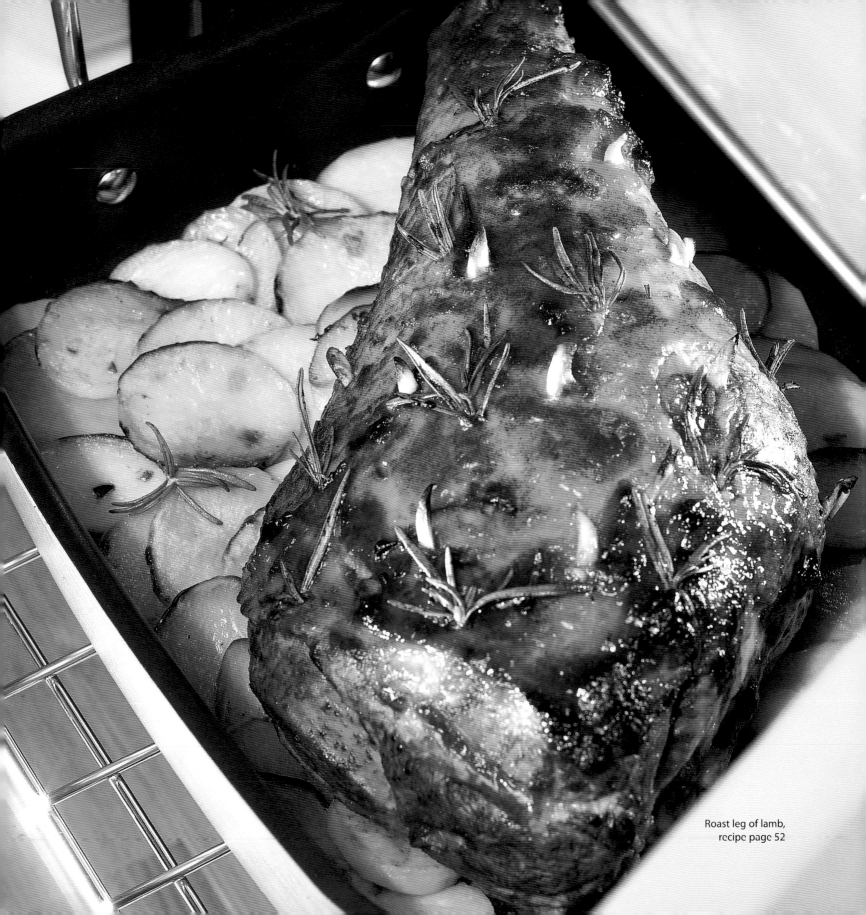

Roast leg of lamb,
recipe page 52

# catalan pork

In this highly seasoned dish, the simplest of ingredients are used to achieve maximum flavour.

Preheat oven to 180°C. Roast pork and potatoes with roughly chopped parsley, salt and pepper and oil for about 20 minutes. Peel and slice 2 large onions and slowly cook over low heat with vegetable oil for ½ hour, add garlic, cook slowly for another ½ hour. Add flour to the onion and garlic mixture and stir over a low heat. Add wine and reduce until onion mixture thickens. Transfer onion mixture to a small tray, lay pork chops and potatoes on top, squeeze the juice of a lemon over the whole lot and bake at 160°C for 20 minutes. To serve, spoon the onions onto a plate with pork chop and potatoes, sprinkle with lots of fresh parsley and serve with warm crusty bread.

6 organic thick pork loin chops
2 large onions
6 medium potatoes, peeled and halved
1 bunch parsley
1 lemon
4–5 cloves garlic
1 tablespoon flour
8fl oz/200ml white wine
Vegetable oil for roasting and frying

**serves 3**

# country ham pie

This recipe was compiled by my pal Sue who helps me with cookery courses. It is an ideal Stephen's Day dish using the leftovers from your traditional Christmas day lunch.

Preheat your oven to 200°C. Roll out half the pastry. Place on a baking tray. Puncture with a fork completely. Bake at 200°C for 15–20 mins. Melt butter. Sauté onion, garlic and leek. Add apple, bay leaf and nutmeg. Add additions if needed. Cook over gentle heat for 15 mins. Remove bay leaf. Cool. Spoon mixture over cooked pastry. Scatter chopped ham over mixture. Lattice the uncooked pastry, eggwash, sprinkle with salt. Wrap over cooked pastry. Cook for about 30–35 mins.

450g/1lb puff pastry
25g/1oz butter/oil
100g/4oz onion finely chopped
1 medium eating apple grated
1 large leek finely sliced
Pinch grated nutmeg
1 bay leaf
25g/1oz plain white flour
300ml/½ pt milk (may add 6 teaspoons white wine/6oz cider and use less milk).
Salt and pepper
2 teaspoons sour cream
200g/8oz chopped cooked ham

**optional additions:**
50g/2oz leftover stuffing
25g/1oz flaked almonds
50g/2oz cooked spinach
50g/2oz cooked beans

**serves 4**

When buying meat, firstly, buy from a known and trusted supplier. Buy organic meat when possible. Meat should look and smell fresh. Look for a good clear colour, this will darken naturally on exposure to the air. The fat on the meat should be creamy white, yellow fat generally indicates that the meat is past its prime. Look for meat with a good amount of "marbling" throughout the meat which will keep it moist during cooking and add flavour.

## sirloin steak with onion marmalade and potato cakes

4 x 175g/6oz thick sirloin steaks
Salt and black pepper
Olive oil
Garlic
125 ml (½ pt) home-made
beef stock
Dash of whiskey
Knob of butter
1 quantity onion marmalade
(see recipe page 119)

**potato cakes**
½ kg (1 lb) potatoes, peeled
and chopped
2–3 tablesp. mixture of milk
and cream (½ & ½ )
Knob of butter
2 tablesp. scallions (spring
onions), chopped
Salt and black pepper

**serves 4/6**

Brush the steaks with oil and season. Cook with some garlic in a hot, heavy bottomed pan to your liking. Do not turn over until the underside is browned, then cook the other side. Remove from the pan and leave to rest. To the juices in the pan, add some beef stock, dash of whiskey, knob of butter and season to taste.

**potato cakes**
Place the potatoes in a large pot. Cover with water. Season, bring to the boil, then simmer until potatoes are cooked. Drain well, then mash really well with the milk, cream and butter. Whip in the scallions, season well. Divide the mixture into four and shape into four potato cakes. Dust each one with a little flour and fry in hot butter until golden brown on each side — keep warm. Place the warm potato cake on the plate with the steak on top. Top the steaks with onion marmalade.

## slow roast belly of pork with caramelised onions & apples

**A rustic, hearty and economical dish that is ideal for the Stanley as it needs to slowcook over a long period of time.**

1 whole pork belly (joint bones
removed), about 2.2lbs/1kg
4 red onions
4 brambly apples

**serves 6**

Pre-heat oven to 180ºC. Finely score the fat side of the belly of pork. Place it in a tray in the bottom of the top oven of your Stanley, after breakfast if you are planning it for lunch. After 1½ to 2 hours, pour off the fat. Peel and slice red onions and apples. Lay them at the bottom of the baking dish and put the pork belly on top, sprinkle with salt and return to the oven. Roast for another 2 hours, until the skin is deliciously crackly, most of the fat has melted and the onions and apples are golden and caramelised, Strain off the juices into a pan and bubble and reduce to a dark brown glaze. To serve, slice the pork belly into thick slices and serve with the caramelised apple and onions. Drizzle with the glaze. Serve with celeriac and potato mash.

"A joint roasted in the Stanley has a crisp golden exterior, sealing in all the natural flavours and juices giving you moist and juicy mouth-watering meat"

# minty lamb stew

This delicious recipe takes literally minutes to assemble using simple ingredients to achieve a hearty flavoursome dish.

Add everything to casserole. Bring to boil, then simmer in the oven at 160°C for 1½ – 2 hours

900g/2lbs diced lamb
2 large onions, sliced
2–3 large tomatoes skinned and chopped*
1–2 large cloves of garlic
Large handful of fresh mint, chopped
Juice of 1 lemon
*I use one tin of tomatoes

**serves 4/6**

# roast leg of lamb

**Recipe by Tim Rooney**

This is my favourite roast dish. I grew up in the west of Ireland and my mum taught me this recipe. We had an old cast iron cooker in the kitchen and there was nothing better than returning from a stormy walk to the smell of the roast in the oven. Now I do the same for my children on an old Stanley 80 in our holiday home in Duncannon.

The preparation is quite simple. Just peel the garlic, stab the leg with a small knife every 1½ inches and place a piece of garlic and a stick of rosemary. Season the leg with salt & pepper and then put in a roasting tray or on your oven spit if you have one and just rub in some oil. Pre heat the oven to 180°C and allow 20 minutes per pound. Take out and leave to rest for 10 minutes before you start to carve. Use the juices to make a gravy (jus). Serve with baby roast potatoes, fresh peas and mint sauce.
Bon Appetit!

1 leg lamb
1 clove garlic
1 bunch rosemary
Salt & freshly ground pepper
Sunflower oil

**serves 6**

Good knives are a kitchen essential. I suggest that you should have the following knives, a small knife with a 4" blade for peeling vegetables, a bread knife with a serrated edge, a filleting knife with a 6" flexible blade for filleting fish, a large knife with a 10" blade for shredding, slicing and chopping, a carving knife for carving meat, a palette knife for spreading and turning food over and most importantly a steel for sharpening your knives.

# lamb tagine

A tasty dish. Subtle spices and the sweetness of the honey and sultanas compliment the delicate flavour of the lamb. Serve a big bowl of baba ganoush (see page 29) as an accompaniment to this dish. The sharp flavour offers a super contrast to the tagine. Serve with couscous.

Preheat the top oven of your Stanley to 180°C. Cut the lamb into 4cm cubes. Place in a bowl with the marinade spices and oil. Season, cover and leave to marinate overnight. Heat 1 tablespoon of oil in a heavy based casserole and brown the lamb in batches. Move the casserole to the simmering ring and add the garlic, chilli and onion and sweat for 5 minutes. Return lamb to the casserole. Stir in flour and tomato purée, then add stock and herbs. Season with salt and pepper. Bring back to the boil, cover and cook at 180°C in the top oven for 1½ hours, stirring occasionally. Remove the bay leaf. Add sultanas and honey and return to oven for 15–20 minutes. Garnish with coriander and serve with couscous. If you prefer a sharper flavour a little lemon juice can be added at the end of cooking to taste.

3lb/1.3kg boneless
shoulder of lamb

**marinade**
2 teaspoons ground ginger
2 teaspoons ground coriander
½ teaspoon turmeric
1 teaspoon cinnamon
Ground salt and pepper
4 tablespoons olive oil

1 tablespoon olive oil
8oz/200g sliced onions
3 garlic cloves, peeled and crushed
½ red chilli, deseeded and finely chopped
1 tablespoon plain flour
2 tablespoons tomato purée
1 pint/500ml chicken stock
4 tablespoons chopped fresh coriander
2 tablespoons chopped fresh parsley
1 bay leaf
75g sultanas
1 tablespoon of local honey
Coriander leaves to garnish

**serves 6**

Mint is the easiest most indestructible herb to grow. In fact it can quite easily become a pest as it tends to grow in front of your eyes! I grow mint very successfully in a big pot. Spearmint is pretty for desserts whilst Eau de cologne mint is great to cook with.

hamburgers with tomato salsa and guacamole, recipe opposite page

# hamburgers with tomato salsa and guacamole

Make these seven days a week and your children will still want more! Serve these burgers in a crispy ciabatta bun with tomato salsa and a big dollop of guacamole ...delicious.

Heat the oil in a frying pan and gently sauté onions until soft. Combine beef, sautéed onion, parsley, salt, beaten egg, oatmeal and freshly milled pepper. Mix well, then shape into burgers. Using the remaining oil sauté the burgers for 5 minutes each side. It is important to cook burgers right through, because the meat is minced there could be a danger of cross-contamination.

If you want to make your burgers even more tasty, push a cube of your favourite cheese into the centre of the burger and cover with mince when shaping.

**hamburgers**
2 tablespoons of sunflower oil
1 finely chopped onion
2lb/900g minced organic beef
(I use round steak)
2 tablespoons of freshly
chopped parsley
Salt and freshly ground pepper
Handful of oatmeal
1 small free range egg beaten

**serves 6**

Mash the avocado flesh in a bowl with the lime cordial and stir in all the other ingredients. Season generously. Cover and refrigerate until ready to use.
*Lime juice can be used instead. I find lime cordial preserves the colour of the avocado and gives a subtle sweet flavour.

**guacamole**
2 large ripe avocados, peeled
and stones removed
2 tablespoons lime cordial*
4 tablespoons crème fraiche
4 ripe tomatoes, skinned
deseeded and chopped
½ red chilli (optional) deseeded
and finely chopped
2 garlic cloves
A dash of tabasco and
Worcestershire sauce
Salt and pepper

In a medium bowl prepare the salsa. Mix the onion, tomato, chilli and coriander. Season. Cover and refrigerate until ready to use.

**tomato salsa**
¼ onion, chopped
1 tomato, chopped
1 chilli, chopped finely
25g/1oz fresh coriander,
chopped
salt and freshly ground black
pepper

# stanley shepherd's pie

**Classic family cooking at its best! Nothing nicer on a cold winter's evening.**

2lbs/900g organic minced beef
2 large onions chopped
3 tablespoons Worcestershire sauce
1 tablespoons tomato purée
3 carrots peeled and diced
1 small glass of red wine
2 sprigs of thyme
Olive oil
Chopped parsley

**For the topping**
3lbs/1.35kg potatoes
4oz/100g butter
½ pint/200ml milk

**serves 4**

Preheat the oven to 180°C. Peel the potatoes, chop each in half and place in a large saucepan of water. Add a teaspoon of salt and bring to the boil. Cook until tender, drain well and return to the pan and add milk, butter, salt and pepper. Mash well and check seasoning. While the potatoes are cooking, put a drop of olive oil in a large casserole, add the onions and fry until softened but not coloured. Add the mince a little at a time and cook until browned. Add the Worcestershire sauce, tomato purée, red wine and thyme. The carrots can be added at this stage and simmer for 25 minutes. Check for seasoning. When cooked place the mince mixture in an oblong ovenproof dish and cover with the mashed potato. Run a fork over the top for decoration. Place in a preheated oven for 20 minutes until the potato is golden brown. Garnish with chopped parsley and serve. (See page 86) for some interesting mash ideas.

# mulled wine beef casserole

**This dish is wonderful at Christmas time, filling your kitchen with its gorgeous mulled wine flavours and aromas. It works well when cooked a day or two in advance of serving.**

1kg rump or lean braising beef
50g/2oz chopped rashers
50g/2oz butter
30ml/2 tablespoons oil
1lb/450g shallots peeled
2 cloves of garlic finely chopped
½ inch of ginger grated
3 heaped tablespoons flour
150ml (¼ pint) beef stock
300ml (½ pint) full bodied red wine
1 cinnamon stick
4 cloves
4 juniper berries
1 diced pear
1 handful cooked chestnuts
1 tablespoon red currant jelly

**serves 4**

Preheat oven to 170°C. Heat oil and butter in a large casserole, add garlic, ginger and shallots and fry gently for five minutes. Add beef and rashers. When beef is browned all over, add flour and stir. Cook for three minutes, then add stock and wine. Bring to the boil and simmer gently for 5 minutes. Put lid on casserole and transfer to oven for 2 hours, stirring occasionally. After two hours add the cinnamon stick, cloves, juniper berries, diced pear, red currant jelly and chestnuts. Cook for a further 15–20 minutes.

# roasting chart

| Type of Meat | Timing per 450g (1lb) | Temperature |
| --- | --- | --- |
| Turkey | Allow 15 minutes per 450g/1lb plus another 20 minutes to finish<br><br>8–12lbs (3.6–5.4kg)    2–3 hours<br>12–16lbs (5.4 – 7.2kg)    3–4½ hours | Cover the turkey with foil and start cooking at 200°C, reducing the temperature to 180°C after 45 minutes. Remove the foil 20 minutes before the end of cooking. |
| Chicken | 20 minutes per lb/450g plus another 15 – 20 minutes to finish, you may need to give a little more time if the bird is very big or less time for a small bird. | Cover the chicken with foil and start cooking at 200°C, reducing the temperature to 180°C after 25 minutes before the end of cooking. |
| Beef | **Beef on the bone cooking times per 450g/1lb:**<br>Rare 10–12 minutes<br>Medium 12–15 minutes<br>Well done 18–20 minutes<br><br>**Beef off the bone cooking times per 450g/1lb:**<br>Rare 8–10 minutes & 15 minutes over<br>Medium 10–12 minutes & 15 minutes over<br>Well done 15–18 minutes & 15 minutes over | Start off roasting at 200°C and reduce the temperature to 180°C after 30–40 minutes. |
| Lamb | **Cooked through:**<br>20 minutes per 450g/1lb & 20 minutes over<br><br>**Cooked pink:**<br>15 minutes per 450g/1lb & 15 minutes over | Start off roasting at 200°C and reduce the temperature to 180°C after 30 minutes. |
| Pork | Pork must always be thoroughly cooked.<br><br>**Pork off the bone:**<br>30 minutes per 450g/1lb & 30 minutes over<br><br>**Pork on the bone:**<br>25 minutes per 450g/1lb & 25 minutes over | Start off roasting at 200°C and reduce the temperature to 180°C after 30 minutes. |

fish

monkfish and mussels poached in a Thai broth, recipe page 65

# baked fillet of cod with hot mango salsa

**This dish works well substituting the cod for salmon. The mango salsa is also perfect accompaniment for grilled or barbecued chicken.**

4 x 175g/6oz fillets of fresh cod
25g/1oz/¼ cup plain flour
1 tablespoon sunflower oil

**hot mango salsa**
1 large ripe mango peeled and cut into ¼"/5mm dice
1 tomato peeled, de-seeded and cut into ¼"/5mm dice
2 red onion, peeled and cut into ¼"/5mm dice
1 garlic clove, finely chopped
1 red chilli de-seeded finely chopped
1 tablespoon fresh coriander leaves, finely chopped
Pinch of chilli powder
Salt and freshly ground pepper
Juice of 1 lime

**serves 4**

Pre-heat oven to 180°C. Combine all the salsa ingredients. Mix well, stir in the lime juice, taste for seasoning. Place in the fridge while cooking the fish. Trim the cod fillets, making sure that all bones are removed. Put the flour in a bowl or dish and dip the skin side of the fillets in the flour. Heat the oil in a pan and when good and hot, sear the cod in the pan, skin side down, for about 2 mins. Remove the fish from the pan (now the skin should be crispy) and put the fish in an ovenproof dish, skin side up this time. Bake in a preheated oven at 180°C for 7–10 mins, until fish is cooked through. When the fish is cooked serve it straight from the oven with a generous spoon of salsa on top. Serve with green salad and wild rice.

# baked salmon with a horseradish crust

**A quick and easy way of making salmon exciting! The crunchy breadcrumbs offer a perfect contrast to the salmon.**

4 darns of salmon
Handful of breadcrumbs
2 oz melted butter
Handful of chopped dill
1 tablespoon of horseradish sauce.

**serves 4**

Preheat the oven to 200°C. Combine the bread crumbs, melted butter and chopped dill. Place salmon skin side down on an oiled tray. Spread horseradish sauce on salmon. Coat with bread crumbs. Bake in preheated oven for 15 minutes. Delicious served with tomato sauce. (see page 117)

*The most important consideration when buying fish is its freshness. Whole fish should have bright, clear eyes, vibrant, shiny skin and vivid pink or red gills. The fish should feel stiff and smell faintly of sea air. Fillets, cutlets and steaks should have translucent flesh and show no signs of discoloration. Ideally fish should be cooked on the day of purchase, but it can be stored well wrapped in your fridge for up to 24 hours. Wild fish is always preferable to farmed fish, ask your supplier to source it for you.*

"The double ovens allow you to roast and bake at the same time, without fear that your baked salmon will interfere with your chocolate pavlova!"

helvick fish pie, recipe opposite page

# helvick fish pie

This is comfort food at its best. The fish you use can be judged to suit the occasion and season. Use cod or salmon as the basis for the mixed fish and include mussels, prawns and monkfish or whatever fish is available at your local fishmongers.

Poach fish in milk with bay leaf until fish is opaque. Strain milk off fish and place fish in pie dish. Melt butter, add flour to make roux, add white wine and stock, whisk until mixture becomes thick. Add reserved milk and whisk until sauce thickens. Season to taste and add chopped dill. Pour sauce over fish, allow to cool. Steam potatoes until cooked. Mash with milk and butter until light and fluffy, season to taste. Smooth mashed potatoes over fish in pie dish. Place in preheated oven 180°C for 15 minutes.

This can be prepared beforehand, chilled and reheated later on that day. A perfect meal served only with a crisp green salad.

1¾lb/800g mixed fish
12fl oz/350ml milk
2fl oz/50ml white wine
2fl oz/50ml chicken stock
1oz/25g butter
1oz/25g flour
Bay leaf
3 sprigs chopped fresh dill
3lbs/1.3kg potatoes, butter and milk for seasoning
Salt and pepper

**serves 4**

# freshly caught mackerel with stewed gooseberries

The sun should never set on mackerel, it should always be used on the day that it is caught. The stewed gooseberries cut beautifully through the oiliness of the fish. Mackerel is also lovely wrapped in tin foil and cooked on the barbecue.

Dissolve the sugar in the water over a gentle heat and bring to the boil. Boil for 2 minutes, then allow to cool. Add the gooseberries to the cooled syrup and bring to the boil, cover and simmer for 1 minute. Take off the heat and allow the gooseberries to cool in the syrup. Heat the frying pan. Dip the fillets in flour, which has been seasoned with salt and pepper. Shake off the excess flour. When the pan is hot add the butter and fry the fillets, the fish should sizzle when they touch the pan. Move the pan away from the hottest part of the hotplate and fry on each side for 4–5 minutes until golden. Serve with stewed gooseberries and a wedge of lemon.

**mackerel**
8 fillets of fresh mackerel
Seasoned flour
Small knob of butter

**stewed gooseberries**
½lb/225g castor sugar
½ pint /225ml water
1lb/450g gooseberries topped and tailed

**serves 4**

*Stewed gooseberries served with greek yoghurt is a lovely summer dessert, add 2 elderflower heads to the syrup for a more interesting flavour.*

# grilled hake with spicy pepperonata, new potatoes and aioli

Recipe by Paul Flynn, Tannery Restaurant, Dungarvan.

The creamy whiteness of the hake contrasts beautifully with the ruddy pepperonata stew. This stew is a particularly good recipe to have in your collection. It goes with virtually everything. Vegetarians love it and the spices give it a little kick that ordinary pepperonata does not have.

**grilled hake**
4x5oz/150g skinless fillets of hake
1 tablespoon crème fraîche
2fl oz/55ml melted garlic butter

**pepperonata sauce**
3 red peppers, seeded
and finely sliced
1 onion, finely sliced
2 garlic cloves, crushed
1 red chilli, seeded and finely
chopped
Olive oil, for frying
Knob butter
Pinch cumin powder
Pinch paprika
Pinch cayenne pepper
Pinch curry powder
100ml strong chicken stock
14oz/400 g can plum tomatoes
puréed
7oz/200 g can white cannellini
beans, drained and rinsed
7oz/200 g can kidney beans,
drained and rinsed
20 black olives (best quality)
Salt and freshly ground black
pepper

**serves 4**

To make the pepperonata sauce, heat the olive oil in a frying pan, add the butter and when it starts to foam sweat the peppers, onion, garlic and chilli for about 10 minutes or until softened. Add the spices and cook for another 3 minutes. Stir in the tomatoes, stock beans and olives and heat gently, stirring to combine and cook for a further 15 minutes. Season and reserve. Pre-heat the grill. Arrange the hake fillets (brushed with garlic butter) on a tray and brush them liberally with crème fraîche. Season and sprinkle the remaining garlic butter over the top of the fish. Cook for 3–4 minutes. To assemble, spoon a pile of pepperonata sauce in the centre of each warm serving plate. Place the hake on top. I would normally serve this with some aioli and basil, new boiled or saffron potatoes or pilaff rice.

# pan-fried scallops and prawns with rocket salad

50g fresh rocket leaves
1 tbsp olive oil
12 shelled king scallops
12 tiger prawns, shells
removed
1 clove garlic, crushed
1" root ginger, peeled and
finely grated
Juice of 1 lemon
2 tablespoons soy sauce
1 tbsp honey

**Serves 4**

Heat the oil in a non stick frying pan over high heat. Add the scallops and cook for about 30 seconds. Add the prawns and once they have turned pink on one side, turn them and the scallops. Cook until the prawns are pink all over and the scallops are just cooked. Transfer to a plate.

Add the remaining ingredients to the pan with 25ml water. Fry over a high heat until the sauce reduces to a thick glaze. Return the prawns and scallops to the pan and toss in the glaze.

Divide the seafood between 4 plates and serve on top of rocket leaves. Pour over any remaining sauce.

Serve immediately.

# monkfish and mussels poached in a thai broth

**This broth is packed full of flavour and is perfect for steaming mussels.**

Cut the monkfish into 1inch/2cm slices and refrigerate until needed. Check the mussels carefully, discarding any broken or open shells. Remove beards and wash well, drain. Heat the oil in a pan (large enough to hold the mussels and monkfish) and add the garlic, shallot, and chilli and fry for a minute or two, add the ginger and lemongrass and fry for another minute. Add the white wine and reduce by two thirds. Add the coconut milk, simmer for a minute or two then add the cream. Add the mussels and monkfish. Cover the pan with the lid and simmer for a few minutes until the mussels are open the monkfish is opaque — about 3–4 minutes. Divide the monkfish and mussels between six warm bowls — I use pasta bowls. Divide the broth between the bowls and scatter the fresh coriander over each. Serve with a wedge of lime and some wild rice.

1¾ lbs/800g monkfish tails, carefully trimmed of skin and membrane.
3lbs/1.3kg mussels
2 tablespoons of sunflower oil
4 cloves of garlic crushed
1 shallot finely chopped
1 red chilli de-seeded and finely chopped
2 stalks of lemongrass finely chopped
1inch/2cm ginger finely grated
6fl oz/150ml dry white wine
14oz/400g of coconut milk
6fl oz/150ml cream
handful of torn coriander leaves
1 lime divided into six wedges

**serves 6**

# lemonsole baked in parchment paper with lemon grass butter

**Cooking fish in parchment paper ensures that all the flavour of the fish is retained during cooking. These little parcels can be made an hour or two in advance and just popped into the oven when required. If you can't get fresh lemongrass, fresh herbs and a knob of butter will do nicely!**

Melt the butter over a low heat in a small pan and add the finely chopped lemongrass. Leave to infuse over a very gentle heat (you don't want the lemongrass to fry). Brush the parchment paper with a little oil. Place the fillets of sole, one on top of the other in the centre of the parchment paper, spooning the lemon grass butter over each fillet and sprinkle with coriander. Season with salt and freshly milled black pepper. Draw opposite sides of the paper together over the fish and fold closed, turn the folded ends underneath. Arrange the fish parcels in one layer on a baking tray. Set the baking tray in the heated oven for 15–20 minutes. To serve place each parcel on a warmed plate and open the parcels just enough to pop in a lemon wedge. Serve this with baby new potatoes and green beans.

8 fillets of lemon sole, skin removed. About 6oz/150g per person
2oz /50g butter
2 finely sliced stalks of lemon grass
4 squares of parchment paper, each one large enough to enclose 2 lemon sole fillets.
1 tablespoon chopped coriander
sunflower oil
4 lime wedges

**serves 4**

*For a delicious paste to serve with fish (either on the side or smeared over grilled fish), whiz a tablespoon of capers, a tablespoon of stoned green olives, a plump clove of garlic and a bunch each of parsley, tarragon and basil. Gradually add enough olive oil to make a paste. Guaranteed to liven up any fish dish!*

poultry and game

chicken Provençal, recipe page 68

# chicken Provençal

A delicious summer stew, judge the amount of chilli you use depending on your family's tolerance to it.
You can make the stew up to a day ahead. Cool completely before covering and chilling. Reheat gently, just to simmering point.

3 tablespoons olive oil
4 chicken drumsticks and
4 chicken thighs
3oz/90g bacon lardons
1 large onion, finely chopped
2 sticks of celery, finely chopped
2 garlic cloves, finely chopped
2 tablespoon plain flour
8 fl oz/250 ml/1 cup white wine
8 fl oz/250 ml/1 cup chicken stock
14oz/400g tin of chopped tomatoes
½ teaspoon chilli powder
2 teaspoons finely chopped fresh rosemary
salt, black pepper

**serves 4**

Put one tablespoon of the oil in a large, shallow, heavy-bottomed pan (it should have a lid), and put on the hot ring of your Stanley, and, when the oil is hot, brown the chicken well on all sides. You will need to do this in batches, because if the pan is too full, the chicken will steam rather than fry. When all the chicken pieces are nicely golden brown, set aside. Pour the fat from the pan and discard. Add the remaining oil to the pan over medium heat and, when it is hot, add the bacon, onion, celery, chilli powder and garlic and cook, stirring occasionally, until the onion is soft, about 10 minutes. Stir in the flour and cook for one minute. Return the chicken pieces to the pan and pour in the wine, stock and tin of tomatoes, sprinkle with rosemary. Bring just to simmering point and put on the lid, move the pan to the simmering ring. Leave to simmer gently for 30 minutes. Take off the lid, turn the chicken pieces and leave to simmer gently, uncovered, for another half an hour, the sauce will thicken slightly. Season to taste with salt and pepper and serve. Garnish with finely chopped fresh rosemary, and serve with wild rice.

# thai green curry

Thigh meat is best for making curry as it more succulent, however some people don't like the brown colour of the thigh meat so breast meat can be used instead.

1 x 220g jar green curry paste
1 red chilli, deseeded and finely chopped
2 cloves of garlic, peeled and crushed
1 inch / 5cm root ginger, peeled and finely grated
1 x 16oz/400ml tin of coconut milk
large bunch of coriander finely chopped, some coriander sprigs for serving
6 x 6oz/125g chicken fillets cut into strips or 1½ lb/900g thigh meat
3 tablespoons of sunflower oil
dash of Rose's lime cordial

**serves 6**

Stir fry the chicken pieces in a hot pan using 2 tablespoons of the oil until golden, remove from pan and set aside. Using the remaining oil fry the chilli, ginger and garlic for a minute. Add half the jar of green curry paste and cook for a further 3 minutes. Add the coconut milk and chopped coriander and simmer for 5 minutes. Add a dash of lime cordial, check seasoning. Add the chicken pieces to the pan and simmer for 20 minutes over a low heat. Serve with some jasmine rice and some chopped coriander.

# marinades for chicken

Here are some simple but yummy marinades to change the flavour of chicken for salads.
Ideal for barbecues!

## ginger grilled chicken

Mix all ingredients and marinate chicken overnight. To cook, butterfly the chicken fillets and cook under a hot grill for 5 minutes each side.

5 fl oz soy sauce
3oz honey
Juice of one lemon
1 tablespoon vegetable oil
1 tablespoon grated fresh ginger
1 clove garlic crushed
4 – 6 chicken fillets

## lemon and rosemary chicken

From one lemon, grate 2 teaspoons of peel. From 2nd lemon, cut thin slices, reserve for garnish. Squeeze juice from remaining 3 lemon halves into a medium bowl. Stir in lemon peel, rosemary, garlic, oil, salt and pepper. Add chicken fillets to lemon juice mixture. Arrange chicken under a medium heat and grill, brushing with remaining lemon juice mixture, for 5 minutes each side until chicken loses its pink colour throughout. Garnish with lemon slices.

2 lemons
1 tablespoon fresh rosemary chopped
1 garlic clove
2 teaspoons olive oil
2 teaspoon salt
2 teaspoon coarsely ground black pepper
4 chicken fillets

## grilled chicken with cumin, coriander and lime

Mix all ingredients and marinate chicken overnight. To cook, butterfly the chicken fillets and cook under a hot grill for 5 minutes on each side.

3 tablespoons fresh lime juice (2 limes)
2 tablespoons olive oil
1 teaspoon ground cumin
1 teaspoon ground coriander
1 teaspoon sugar
1 teaspoon salt
pinch ground red pepper
4 chicken fillets

# pheasant and apple casserole

Use the fillets for this recipe, the bones can be used to make delicious game stock. This casserole is even better when prepared a day before, giving the flavours a chance to develop.

6 pheasant fillets, skin removed
4 streaky bacon rashers, chopped
Seasoned flour (2 dessert spoons of flour seasoned with salt, freshly milled black pepper and mustard powder)
1 tablespoon plain flour
4 medium cooking apples, peeled and sliced
6–8 dried prunes
2 onions, peeled and chopped
2oz/50g butter
½ pint/275ml strong dry cider
7fl oz/200ml crème fraîche
¼ pint/150ml chicken stock

**serves 4**

Toss the pheasant fillets in the seasoned flour. Peel and core the apples and cut into slices. Melt the butter in a heavy casserole and brown the pheasant fillets. Remove and set aside. Add the chopped bacon to the casserole and fry until golden. Add the onions, prunes and apple and cook until the onions have softened, about 10 minutes. Stir in a tablespoon of flour and cook for a couple of minutes. Add the stock and cider, blend and bring to the boil. Return the pheasant fillets to the casserole and simmer with the lid on for about 15/20 minutes. Just before serving, spoon in the crème fraîche.

# rabbit with cabbage, gin and juniper

This amazing recipe was given to me by County Waterford's most fabulous hostess, Suzanne Holmes!

1 rabbit
1 spanish onion
2 cloves of garlic
250ml dry cider
1 savoy cabbage
1 tablespoon juniper berries
2 tablespoons cornflour
Good slug of gin

**serves 2**

Section the rabbit (two pieces per person) or use saddles only which you can buy frozen and are meatier. Alternatively, you could also use chicken for this but rabbit has a more elusive gamey flavour. Roll rabbit in seasoned flour and brown in good olive oil in a large frying pan. Keep warm. In the same pan gently cook one large sliced Spanish onion until lightly coloured. Add two cloves of chopped garlic and cook on for another minute. Add enough strong dry cider to cover onion mixture and cook gently for about five minutes to soften onion and absorb. Meanwhile quarter a large Savoy (or other dense cabbage) or if very large cut into wedges about two inches thick. Put wedges into boiling water for four minutes and then drain well. Lightly crush three tablespoons of juniper berries (put in a plastic bag and tap gently with a hammer ) or use a pestle and mortar if you have this.

Mix two tablespoons cornflour with a good slug of gin (a double!). In a large mixing jug, dissolve two chicken stock cubes in a little boiling water. Add cornflour mixture and a bottle of the strong cider plus the juniper berries and pour the lot over the onions. Stir well and simmer gently for 3 – 4 minutes. Arrange cabbage in a large casserole or pot with lid. Place rabbit on top and pour over onions and sauce. Top up with a bit more cider if necessary to cover rabbit. Scrunch up a piece of wet greaseproof paper and place over the top and put on casserole lid. The paper makes a tight seal if the lid does not fit well. Cook in oven at lowest temperature for about six hours. Serve with creamy mash. The cabbage will still be in its nice wedge shape and both cabbage and rabbit will melt in the mouth. Some of the grandest people have raved about this dish!

# roast duck with plum sauce

A free-range duck is ideal. Try to find a local supplier who will find you a nice plump duck that will feed four people comfortably. Plan ahead as you may need to order this in advance.

Preheat the oven to the hottest setting. Boil the kettle and pour the boiling water over the duck, then dry thoroughly. Score the duck crown with a sharp knife at 1cm spaces and place on a wire rack on a roasting tray. Brush the duck with honey, salt and pepper, place it in hot oven and roast at high temperature for 30 minutes. Baste the duck regularly during cooking so that it develops a rich glaze. After 30 minutes drain off some of the fat and return to the oven, reducing the temperature to 180°C for another half an hour. Baste regularly and cover if browning too quickly. Remove from oven and allow to rest for 15–20 minutes in a warm place. To make the plum sauce, combine all the ingredients in a small saucepan. Bring to the boil and simmer for 10 minutes, or until mixture starts to collapse. This sauce may be served hot or cold. I like to make it a day or so in advance to allow the flavours to infuse.

Delicious served with Celeriac Pommes Anna. (see page 89)

**roast duck**
1 x 1900g/4lb duck
2 tablespoons of honey
Freshly ground salt and pepper

**plum sauce**
8oz/200g stoned plums
5oz/125g50g (2oz) castor sugar
Juice of one orange
1 teaspoon of chopped shallots
1 clove garlic peeled and chopped
2.5cm/1 inch cinnamon bark
1 star anise
1 glass port

**serves 3/4**

# confit duck legs

The slow steady heat of the simmering ring of your Stanley cooker is ideal for this dish, which needs heat consistency. The more confit you can prepare the better as you can remove them from the fat as you need them. I buy my organic duck legs from the English Market in Cork, enquire locally to access your nearest supplier, you may need to order in advance.

Duck Confit is best prepared in a large stockpot or ham pot so that the fat can't bubble over the rim and be a potential fire hazard. First of all you need to marinade the duck legs over night. Don't be put off by the amount of fat/oil used, this can be reused up to six times. Marinade the duck legs overnight in a container covered with cling film. Place the duck legs and the marinade ingredients in a large pot with enough oil to cover the duck. Simmer very gently on a low heat for two hours. Allow to cool. Transfer to a container large enough to hold the duck legs and refrigerate until needed. Pluck the confit duck legs from the fat when needed. To serve scrape the excess fat from the duck and panfry or roast until crispy. Confit duck marries well with potato and Celeriac Pommes Anna, or gratin potatoes and a carrot and celeriac mash. (see page 85-89)

12 duck legs
Bunch of thyme, parsley, rosemary, sage or whatever herbs you have at hand
10 juniper berries
½ cinnamon stick
4 cloves of garlic
1 onion chopped
A dessertspoon of rock salt
Peel of 2 oranges and 1 lemon (the addition of citrus is essential to cut through the oil)
3½ – 5 pints/2–3 litres, the duck needs to be covered in oil, the amount you use depends on the size of the pot you cook the duck legs in

**serves 12**

# talking turkey

As a child I was advised by my mother not to discuss religion or politics, as an adult who gives Christmas cookery classes, I add turkey to that list. If you want a heated argument , in fact one that has the potential to turn nasty …try talking turkey! From cooking on the bone, to off the bone, slow roast, hot roast, to stuff or not to stuff. I could go on forever…

I try to buy free range or better still organic turkey over battery reared turkey, the flavour of the organic bird is far superior to that of its battery reared counterpart. You will probably need to source an organic turkey and order it well in advance of when you need it. If you purchase your turkey a day or two in advance, make sure you have adequate fridge space to store it before cooking. Some people choose to bone and roll their turkey, this makes carving much easier, but I feel that some of the flavour is lost this way and you must be very careful to keep the bird moist during cooking as it can tend to dry out.

The rule of thumb when cooking turkey is allow 15 to 20 minutes per lb and 15 minutes over. Weigh your turkey and work out the cooking time. A 12–14 lb turkey will feed a family of 6 for 2 days, there is a chance that a bird larger than this could dry out a little as the overall cooking time gets longer.

I prefer to stuff the cavity and cover the turkey breast and legs with muslin soaked in half stock and half melted butter. Start it off in a hot oven at 200°C for the first 45 minutes, then reduce the temperature to 170°C for the rest of the cooking time. The muslin can be removed 20 minutes before the end of cooking if you want the skin to be crisp. Check the juices between the thigh and carcass. When the juices run clear you know that your turkey is cooked.

Allow to relax for at least half an hour before carving. Turning the turkey upside whilst relaxing ensures that juices return to the breast.

# stuffing for turkey

Sweat the onions gently in the butter until soft. Transfer to a large bowl and stir in the rest of the ingredients. Season well. Allow to cool. Dry the cavity of the bird with some kitchen paper and half fill with the cold stuffing. Fill the neck end with the remainder of the stuffing.

12oz/350g onions finely chopped
6oz/175g butter
1lb/450g soft white breadcrumbs
2oz/50g freshly chopped herbs such as thyme, parsley, marjoram and sage
3oz/75g crispy bacon
Grated rind of one orange
Salt and freshly milled pepper

**serves 12**

vegetarian

cherry tomato and garlic cream cheese tarts with pesto, recipe page 76

# beetroot risotto with boilie cheese

**Beetroot gives this dish a wonderfully vibrant colour. The flavour of the Boilie cheese is a perfect contrast to the sweetness of the beetroot.**

1oz/25g butter
1 onion, peeled and finely chopped
1 garlic clove, peeled and sliced
8oz/225g arborio rice
Salt and pepper
1¼ pints/750ml vegetable stock
2–3 cooked baby beetroot
4 tablespoons freshly grated parmesan cheese
Extra parmesan cheese to serve
8 balls of Boilie cheese

**serves 4**

Melt the butter in a heavy-based saucepan. Add the onion and garlic and cook for about 5 minutes or until the onion is beginning to soften. Add the rice, salt and pepper and cook stirring, for about 2 minutes. Add just enough stock to cover the rice and continue cooking, stirring all of the time until most of the stock has been absorbed , continue adding the stock in this way until it is completely absorbed and the rice is tender. Liquidise the beetroot with some freshly milled salt and black pepper, stir beetroot into the rice. Heat through for 1–2 minutes. Remove from the heat and stir in the parmesan. Adjust the seasoning and serve immediately, with 2 balls of Boilie cheese on each portion.

Boilie cheese is a soft hand made cows milk cheese preserved in sunflower oil, flavoured with fresh garden herbs. Boilie is made in Co. Cavan and is available in most supermarkets.

# mushroom and pasta gratin

**A quick and filling light dinner or supper, children love the creamy sauce and pasta shells.**

8oz/200g dried pasta shells
Salt and freshly ground pepper
2 teaspoons olive oil
25g/1oz butter
460g/1lb button mushrooms, halved or quartered
75ml/3fl oz brandy (optional)
1 tablespoon chopped fresh tarragon
1 tablespoon chopped fresh chives
300ml/½ pint double cream
50g/2oz fresh parmesan, freshly grated

**serves 4**

Cook pasta in a large pan of boiling water until al dente. Drain and immediately refresh under cold water, then drain well and toss with a little oil to prevent sticking. Melt the butter in a large frying pan, add the mushrooms and stir fry for 4–5 minutes until golden. Add the brandy (if using) and boil rapidly until only 2 tablespoons of liquid remains. Stir in the chopped herbs and remove from heat. Toss the mushrooms with the pasta and transfer to a lightly oiled gratin dish. Mix the cream with half of the parmesan and pour over the pasta. Sprinkle the remaining cheese on top and bake at 190°C for 20–25 minutes until golden and bubbling.

# cherry tomato and garlic cream cheese tarts drizzled with pesto

**Very impressive for minimal effort, these tasty tarts are delicious al fresco with a glass of white wine.**

9oz/225g ready made puff pastry
3oz/75g cream cheese with garlic – boursin is perfect
Beaten egg to glaze
2 tablespoons of good quality pesto
10 ripe cherry tomatoes (organic or homegrown for best flavour)

**serves 4**

Preheat the oven to 200°C. Cut cherry tomatoes in half and season with salt and freshly milled pepper. On a floured surface, roll the pastry to a rectangular shape. Trim the edges and divide into four rectangular pieces about 4 x 6 inches/10 x 15 cm. Lay the puff pastry pieces on a baking tray, not touching each other. Chill for 20 minutes. Spread a quarter of the garlic cheese into the centre of the puff pastry piece. Arrange 5 cherry tomato halves over the cheese base. Turn in the edges of each pastry piece pinching the corners to make a box shape. Brush the edges with the beaten egg. Bake in the oven at 200°C for 15–20 minutes. Serve warm drizzled with pesto.

beetroot risotto with Boilie cheese, recipe opposite page

Spanish omelette, recipe opposite page

# spanish omelette

This omelette is filled with al dente slices of potato and has a delicate saffron flavour. The roasted vegetables bring colour, flavour and texture to the dish.

Bring a pan of salted water to the boil then add the sliced potatoes, bring back to the boil and simmer for 8 minutes. Heat 1 tablespoon of the oil in a frying pan, around 25cm in diameter, over a medium heat. Add the potato slices and cook until golden – about 10 minutes. Remove from the pan, add the remaining 1 tablespoon of oil and reduce the heat slightly. Add the onion and cook until soft but not coloured. Lightly beat the eggs, add the saffron strands along with the steeping liquid. and season. Return the potato slices to the pan with the onions and peppers and stir to mix. Pour in the beaten eggs and cook over a low heat until set and golden on the base. Once set, loosen the tortilla around the edges with a spatula. Put a large plate over the pan and tip the pan upside down so that the omelette falls on to the plate, then slide the omelette back into the pan, uncooked side down, and cook for a further few minutes until golden on the other side. Transfer to a plate and cut into squares. Serve warm with a green salad.

12oz/300g maris piper or other waxy potatoes, scrubbed and cut into 5mm slices
2 tablespoons olive oil
1 medium red onion, finely sliced
6 medium free range eggs
1 roast red and 1 roast yellow pepper deseeded and cut into strips
Pinch of saffron, steeped in 1 tablespoon freshly boiled water
Salt and freshly ground pepper

**serves 2**

# pasta with delicious variations on tomato sauce

Homemade tomato sauce (see page 117) is really handy to have in your fridge. It is so versatile and appeals to all tastes. Varying the accompanying ingredients can totally change its flavour and usage. Send students back to college armed with oodles of tomato sauce and the following recipes and you need never worry about their diet.

# spaghetti with tomato, basil and crème fraîche

Add the pasta to a saucepan of boiling water, stir as the water reboils and cook for 6–8 minutes until al dente, then drain. Warm the tomato sauce until hot. Add the hot pasta to the tomato sauce (see page 120), stir in the crème fraîche and basil leaves. Divide between four pasta bowls and sprinkle grated Parmesan on top. Serve with focaccia bread.

1 quantity of tomato sauce (see page 120)
250ml tub of crème fraîche
Handful of basil leaves
10oz /250g spaghetti
1 tablespoon olive oil

**serves 2**

# roast mediterranean vegetables with penne

Warm ratatouille to simmering point. Cook penne as in recipe above and add to the hot ratatouille (see page 120). To serve divide between four pasta bowls and sprinkle grated Parmesan on top.

10oz/250g penne
1 quantity of tomato sauce (see page 120)
1 quantity mediterranean ratatouille. (see page 93)

**serves 2**

# goat's cheese & tomato penne

1 quantity tomato sauce
(see page 120)
100g/4oz goat's cheese, I use
"chevre" as it amalgamates well
with the tomato sauce
10oz/250g penne
1 roasted red pepper (skin and
seeds removed)

**serves 2**

Warm the tomato sauce gently on the simmering plate. Add the goat's cheese and roast red pepper and stir until the goat's cheese starts to soften. Stir sauce into al dente pasta. For an extra kick caramelised onions are delicious stirred into this sauce.

# vegetable tagine with rocket and yoghurt sauce

**This has a wonderfully aromatic flavour. The following recipe serves four as a main course or six as an accompaniment to lamb.**

5 tablespoons golden olive oil
2 medium onions peeled and
thinly sliced
2 garlic cloves, peeled and
finely chopped
2 red peppers de-seeded and
thinly sliced
½ red chilli de-seeded and
finely chopped
2 teaspoons ground coriander
2 teaspoons paprika
1 teaspoon each ground
cumin, cinnamon, and turmeric
¼ teaspoon cayenne pepper
14oz/400g tin of chickpeas
14oz/400g tin chopped
tomatoes
½ pint/300ml vegetable stock
1 large aubergine, diced
8oz/200g mushrooms, halved
3oz/75g ready to eat dried
apricots
Salt and freshly milled pepper

**to serve**
8oz/200g couscous
Small bunch of chopped
coriander
1oz/25g flaked almonds
4 oz /100g rocket leaves

**serves 4**

Heat 2 tablespoons of the oil in a frying pan, add the onion, garlic, chilli, red pepper and spices and fry over a medium heat for 5 minutes until golden. Using a slotted spoon, transfer to a saucepan; add the chickpeas and their liquid, tomatoes and stock. Heat another 3 tablespoons of oil in the frying pan and add the aubergine and fry, stirring, over a high heat for 5 minutes until evenly browned. Add the aubergine to the chickpea mixture. Bring to the boil, cover and simmer gently for 15–20 minutes. Heat the remaining oil in the frying pan and stir-fry the mushrooms for 4–5 minutes until browned, then add to the stew with the roughly chopped apricots and cook for a further 10 minutes. Check seasoning. Cook couscous according to instructions. For the yoghurt and cumin sauce, mix the yoghurt, cumin seeds and garlic. Season with salt and pepper. Pile the couscous onto warmed plates and top with the tagine. Scatter over the toasted almonds and chopped coriander, pile rocket leaves on top, and drizzle with the yoghurt sauce and serve at once.

**yoghurt and cumin sauce**
8fl oz/200ml greek yoghurt,
thinned with 2 tablespoons milk
1 garlic clove, crushed to
a paste with salt
1½ teaspoons cumin seeds
roughly ground.

"The subtle warmth rising from your Stanley is perfect for drying herbs. Hang little bunches of herbs over your Stanley, and have them near to hand to use as they dry out"

vegetables

winter red cabbage salad, recipe page 43

gratin dauphinois, recipe page 85

# chickpeas with spinach

This is a super accompaniment for a curry or indeed any traditional Indian food.

Drain the chickpeas and rinse under cold water. Peel and finely chop ginger. Peel and crush garlic. Immerse the tomatoes in boiling water for 30 seconds, then remove and peel away the skins. Finely chop the tomato flesh. Trim and chop the spinach and tear the fresh coriander. Heat the oil in a heavy-based saucepan. Add the ginger, garlic and spices and cook for two minutes, stirring all the time. Add the chickpeas and stir to coat in the spice mixture. Add the tomatoes, fresh coriander and spinach. Cook for 2 minutes, then cover with a lid and simmer gently for 10 minutes. Season with salt and pepper. Garnish with coriander.

Two 14oz/400g cans of chick peas
Salt and pepper
1 inch fresh root ginger
3 garlic cloves
4 tomatoes
450g/1lb spinach leaves
Handful fresh coriander
2fl oz/50ml oil
2 teaspoons ground coriander
1 teaspoon ground cumin
2 teaspoons paprika
Coriander sprigs to garnish

**serves 4**

# gratin dauphinois

The secret of this dish's creamy sauce is not to wash the potatoes which retains the starch, giving a thick, rich sauce.

Preheat oven to 150°C. Butter a 12 inch shallow gratin/oven proof dish. Peel the potatoes and slice them thinly. Place the potatoes with the milk, cream, garlic, salt and pepper into a large saucepan and bring to the boil. Allow to boil for 2–3 minutes and then transfer to the buttered dish. Place dish in the oven for 50 minutes, until cooked.

2.2lbs/1kg good quality potatoes
2 cloves of garlic crushed
10 fl oz/cream
10 fl oz/milk
Salt and freshly milled pepper

**serves 4**

# delicious mashes

Here are some suggestions for inspirational uses for the humble spud!

## lemon and mustard mash

2.2lbs/1 kg potatoes, halved
2 oz/60g butter
grated zest of 1 lemon
1 tablespoon lemon juice
2 tablespoon grainy mustard
4 tablespoon double (heavy) cream
milk
Salt, black pepper, grated nutmeg

**serves 4**

Put the potatoes in a large pan of cold salted water. Bring to the boil and, with the lid on, simmer steadily (rather than boiling hard) until tender – check after 20 minutes. Drain and then put back in the dry pan over a low heat to steam out any wateriness. Using a potato masher, mash to a smooth purée, then beat in the butter, lemon zest and juice, mustard and cream, drizzling in a little milk as needed to achieve the consistency of a thick purée. Keep beating until the potatoes are really light and fluffy. Season to taste and serve at once.

## celeriac & potato mash

1 celeriac peeled and cubed
2.2lbs/1kg potatoes peeled and cubed
2oz/50g butter
3 tablespoons creamy milk
Salt and freshly milled black pepper

**serves 4**

Steam the potatoes and celeriac together until soft. Heat the butter and milk with salt and pepper. Mash the potato and celeriac with the butter and milk mixture until smooth. Stir in chopped parsley and serve hot. The celeriac can be substituted with carrots.

## colcannon

½ head of spring cabbage
2.2lbs/1kg potatoes
2oz/50g butter
3 tablespoons creamy milk
Salt and freshly milled black pepper

**serves 4**

Steam the potatoes until soft. Wash and shred the cabbage leaves and plunge in pot of salted boiling water, cook until soft and drain. Heat the butter and milk with salt and pepper. Mash the potato with the butter and milk mixture until smooth. Stir in the cabbage and serve hot.

honey and soy roast carrots and parsnips, recipe opposite page

# pommes anna with celeriac

Preheat the oven to 190°C. Melt the butter in a heavy pan. Peel the potatoes and slice as thinly as possible – a mandolin works well. Don't put the potato into water as this will wash away the starch and prevent the cake sticking together. Peel and thinly slice the celeriac. Baseline a 25cm (10in) loose-based cake tin with parchment and brush with melted butter. Layer up the potato and celeriac slices, slightly overlapping, seasoning well with salt, freshly ground black pepper and nutmeg at each layer. Finish by drizzling with butter and seasoning generously again. Cover with parchment, then put a 23cm (9in) cake tin filled with baking beans on top to compact the cake, making it easier to slice. Bake for 1hr 10min or until potatoes are tender. Cool, cover and chill overnight. To heat up, invert tin on to a heatproof serving plate and warm in the oven at 190°C for 10 min, then brown under a preheated grill for 5–10min. Serve sliced into wedges.

6oz/175g unsalted butter
2lb/900g potatoes
1 celeriac head – about
1½lb/700g
Freshly grated nutmeg

**serves 6**

# honey and soy roast carrots and parsnips

**Scrub rather than peel the vegetables and choose small to medium sized vegetables for a sweet flavour.**

Preheat the oven to 200°C. Scrub the carrots and parsnips and cut in half, I usually divide the top half in two, you want the vegetables to be equal in size so that they will cook evenly. Mix the honey, olive oil and soy, season and marinade the vegetables for an hour. Put the vegetables and marinade into a hot roasting dish and roast in a hot oven for 20 minutes, turning occasionally, until al dente and golden. Serve hot.

5 medium sized organic carrots
5 medium sized organic parsnips
2 tablespoons of runny honey
2 tablespoons soy sauce
2 tablespoons olive oil
Salt and freshly milled pepper

**serves 6**

# pan-fried turnip and bacon

**A tasty way of preparing this traditional root vegetable when it comes into season late in the year.**

Peel and dice the turnip and steam until al dente. Heat a dessert spoon of sunflower oil in a non stick frying pan until hot but not smoking. Fry the lardons until golden, and set aside on some kitchen paper. Wipe out the pan with some kitchen paper and add a dessert spoon of sunflower to the pan, again heat the oil until hot and add the turnip, fry until golden. Add the lardons to the pan and fry for a further 2 minutes Season and serve hot.

1 medium sized turnip
3oz/75g bacon lardons
Sunflower oil
Salt and freshly milled pepper

**serves 6**

# roast mediterranean vegetables

**Ratatouille is very versatile. It can be used as an addition to pasta, pizza topping, filling for vol au vents, or as a vegetable accompaniment for meat, fish and poultry.**

12oz/300g courgettes, roughly chopped *
1lb/400g red and yellow peppers deseeded and chopped *
12oz /300g aubergines, roughly chopped *
2 red onions cut into chunks *
Olive oil
1 quantity of tomato sauce (See page 120)

**serves 6**

Lightly coat the vegetables in olive oil and place on a baking sheet, keeping the different types separate. Roast in an oven preheated to 180°C gas mark 4 – the courgettes for 10 minutes, the peppers and onions for 15 minutes and the aubergines for 20 minutes. Remove from the oven. Add tomato sauce to make ratatouille.

*Cut the vegetables according to their end use, i.e. small dice for vol au vents.

*Always taste food as you cook. Flavours of ingredients change according to the time of year, where they were grown or in the case of meat where it was reared and who is cooking it. Changes in the method of cooking can alter the flavour of a dish even when the ingredients are kept the same. Keep tasting to check for sweetness, sharpness and spiciness. Season according to your own taste.*

"The hotplate offers rapid boiling at one end perfect for fast boiling root vegetables, and gentle simmering at the other end where you can melt chocolate beautifully and warm your before bed cup of milk"

## buying vegetables

Vegetables are best eaten when in season. Buy local organic vegetables when at all possible. Your local farmer's market is the ideal place to buy your vegetables as you know exactly where they were grown and by whom. Don't be afraid to experiment with new unfamiliar vegetables, take note of the varieties you buy and compare flavours when you cook. Have an open mind when going to buy your vegetables, and choose the freshest looking produce. In the ideal world vegetables should be bought and used on a daily basis.

## cooking vegetables

Vegetables should, as much as possible, be eaten in their raw state, however some vegetables have to be cooked to aid digestion and make them more palatable. Steaming, boiling and roasting are the principal ways of cooking vegetables.

When boiling your vegetables put them into a large pot of vigorously boiling water and cook uncovered until al dente. (this method is ideal for broccoli, beans and peas). Some vegetables require only a little water in a covered saucepan (i.e. carrots, cauliflower and celery).

Steaming is perfect for spinach, which requires very little cooking, and root vegetables which require more cooking, as we don't want to lose all the nutrients in the cooking water.

Roasting is ideal for root vegetables and peppers as they caramelise and sweeten whilst cooking. Use the best quality olive oil available to you when roasting vegetables.

When vegetables are cooked properly very little else in the way of seasoning is needed, just a little salt and freshly milled pepper and in some instances a sprinkling of fresh herbs.

# vegetable calender

**january** — Jerusalem artichokes, beetroot, brussels sprouts. Cabbage (green, red, white), carrots, celeriac, chard, chicory, curly kale, leeks, mushrooms, onions, parsnips, potatoes, spring greens, swede, turnips.

**february** — Jerusalem artichokes, beetroot, brussels sprouts. Cabbage (green, red, white), carrots, celeriac, chard, chicory, curly kale, leeks, mushrooms, onions, parsnips, potatoes, spring greens, swede, turnips and watercress

**march** — Jerusalem artichokes, beetroot, purple sprouting broccoli, brussels sprouts. Cabbage (green, red, white), carrots, cucumber, chard, chicory, leeks, mushrooms, onions, parsnips, potatoes, spring greens, swede, turnips and watercress

**april** — Beetroot, purple sprouting broccoli, cabbage (spring, green), carrots, cucumber, leeks, mushrooms, potatoes, radishes, sorrel, spinach, spring greens, swede and watercress

**may** — Asparagus, purple sprouting broccoli, cucumber, mushrooms, potatoes, radishes, rocket, sorrel, spinach, spring greens, spring onions and watercress

**june** — Asparagus, broad beans, broccoli, new season carrots, celery, courgettes, cucumbers, pickling gherkins, lettuce, peas, new potatoes, radishes, rocket, sorrel, spinach, spring onions and new season turnips.

**july** — Globe artichokes, beans (broad, french, runner) broccoli, new season carrots, celery, chard, courgettes, cucumbers, lettuce, peas, new potatoes, radishes, rocket, sorrel, spinach, spring onions, tomatoes and turnips.

**august** — Globe artichokes, beans (broad, french, runner), beetroot, broccoli, carrots, celery, chard, courgettes, cucumbers, leeks, lettuce, marrows, mushrooms, pickling onions, peas, new potatoes, radishes, rocket, sorrel, shallots, spinach, spring onions, tomatoes and turnips.

**september** — Globe artichokes, beans (french, runner), beetroot, broccoli, carrots, celery, chard, chicory, courgettes, cucumbers, leeks, lettuce, marrows, mushrooms, onions, new and maincrop potatoes, pumpkins, radishes, rocket, shallots, sorrel, spinach, spring onions, swede, sweetcorn, tomatoes, turnips and watercress.

**october** — Beans (french, runner), beetroot, broccoli, cabbage (red, green, savoy), celeriac, chicory, chard, leeks, lettuce, marrows, mushrooms, onions, maincrop potatoes, pumpkins, radishes, rocket, shallots, spinach, onions, swede, sweetcorn, turnips and watercress

**november** — Beetroot, broccoli, brussels sprouts, cabbage (red, green, savoy), celeriac, chard, chicory, mushrooms, onions, maincrop potatoes, parsnips, pumpkins, shallots, spinach, swede, turnips and watercress

**december** — Jerusalem artichokes, beetroot, brussels sprouts, cabbage (green, red, white), celeriac, chard, chicory, curly kale, leeks, mushrooms, onions, parsnips, potatoes, swede and turnips.

bread and baking

# powersfield house brown bread

This is a buttermilk recipe. The Stanley is wonderful for making brown bread, as the even heat puffs up the wheat and gives the loaf a golden glow.

10 oz extra coarse wholemeal flour
55g / 2 oz oatmeal
6 oz Self raising flour
1 tsp soda
1 level tsp salt
'dollop' of sunflower oil
500ml buttermilk (at room temperature)
A tablespoon of pumpkin and sunflower seeds

**makes 2lb loaf**

Mix self raising flour, sieved bread soda and salt into a large mixing bowl. Add the brown flour and oatmeal. Measure the buttermilk into a large measuring jug and add a 'dollop' of oil (to make approx 550ml fluid, no more!) Mix this into dry ingredients and pour into oiled loaf tin.
Sprinkle pumpkin and sunflower seeds on the top (optional). Bake in pre-heated oven at 200°C / 400°F / Gas mark 6 for 40 – 45 minutes. Turn out onto rack to cool.

# yeast bread/focaccia/pizza base

This is a fabulously versatile recipe which makes delicious soft yeast bread or can be adapted to make foccacia or a thin and crispy base for pizzas. Children love to make their own pizzas!

700g (1.2lb) strong plain white flour
Pinch salt
1 × 7g sachet dried yeast
450ml (w pint) warmed water
3 tablespoons olive oil
Coarse sea salt for sprinkling
A few sprigs of rosemary

Sift flour, salt and yeast into a large bowl. Make a well in the centre and pour in the warm water and the olive oil to form soft dough. Knead for 10 minutes until smooth and elastic, then place in a greased bowl. Cover with a cloth and leave to rise in a warm place for 1½–2 hours until doubled in size*. Knock back the dough and divide into two pieces. Roll out into two 10 inch circles and place on greased baking sheets. Cover with damp cloth and leave to rise for 30 minutes. Using your fingers make deep dimples in the dough and drizzle olive oil in the dimples, sprinkle with rock salt, rosemary and spray with water. Bake at 200°C for 20–25 minutes, spraying with water twice during cooking. Transfer to a wire rack to cool. Serve warm if possible or on the same day.

Note. *Cover bowl with cling film to speed up rising.

# white yeast bread

Use recipe as above. To make a loaf of white bread, when the dough has been knocked back after rising, place the dough into an oiled 2lb loaf tin. Allow to rise beside your Stanley for half an hour, or until the dough rises above the level of the tin. Brush with egg wash and bake at 200°C for 30 minutes or until the bread has risen and sounds hollow when tapped underneath.

# pizza base

Use recipe as above. To make pizza base, when the dough has been knocked back after rising. Divide into six pieces and roll out thinly and place on oiled baking trays. Spread tomato sauce (see page 117) and place toppings on top, bake for 7–10 minutes at 200°C.

"The gentle warmth released by the Stanley is ideal for rising and proving bread and the oven is perfect for baking"

stanley scones, recipe opposite page

# stanley scones

**Perfect for breakfast and teatime and a popular addition to the school lunch box .**

Preheat the oven to 220°C. Sieve the flour and baking powder into a bowl and stir in the castor sugar, mix well. Cut the butter into little pieces and rub into the dry ingredients. Beat the eggs and milk together and add the to dry ingredients, keeping enough of the milk/egg mixture back to use as egg wash. Mix well until soft dough is formed. Knead into a ball shape. Using a rolling pin, roll the dough until it is 1-inch thick. Stamp out scones with scone cutter. Place scones on a baking tray. Brush scones with egg wash and sprinkle the scones with poppy seeds if available. Bake in the oven for 10 minutes until golden on top. Cool on a wire rack. Delicious served warm with butter and home-made jam. (see page 119)

1lb/450g plain flour
1 dessert spoon of castor sugar
1 dessert spoon baking powder
3oz/75g butter
2 free range eggs
8fl oz/200ml milk
Pinch of salt

**makes 12**

# shortbread

Preheat oven to 160°C/325°F. Mix together the flour and salt. Cut the butter into pieces and rub in to resemble breadcrumbs. Add the sugar, semolina and orange rind and continue to rub until the mixture forms a ball. Gently pat out the ball with your hand to a thickness of 5mm (1/4 "). Cut into shapes with a cutter. Place on a lined baking tin and place in the centre of the oven for approximately 20 minutes until very pale golden.

Serve with fresh cream or ice-cream and strawberries.

115g/4oz plain flour
¼ teaspoon salt
55g/2oz semolina
55g/2oz caster sugar
115g/4oz butter
grated rind of an orange

# chocolate celebration cake

**This is the perfect cake for a celebration, afternoon tea or dessert. It is a very simple cake to whip up using simple store cupboard ingredients. Children love decorating it for their own parties — just be prepared for very original-looking results!**

Preheat oven to 170°C. Line the base of a 10" tin with a disc of greaseproof paper and grease the sides of the tin with butter. Using an electric mixer beat the eggs and caster sugar with a tablespoon of lukewarm water for 10 minutes until mixture is thick and creamy and doubled in size. Twice sieve the cocoa powder and plain flour. Using a metal spoon gently fold the cocoa and flour into the mixture. Pour the mixture into the prepared tin and place in pre heated oven. Bake for 20 minutes or until cake starts to come away from the sides of the tin. Remove the cake from the tin and allow to cool on a cooling rack. When cool split the cake in two halves.

**For the chocolate glaze** melt the chocolate and butter together over gentle heat until both butter and chocolate combine. Remove from heat.

**To assemble the cake** whip the cream for the filling until soft peaks form; add a dessert spoon of castor sugar and a dessert spoon of liqueur if desired. Spread the whipped cream on the bottom half of the cake; arrange the fruit on top. Cover with the top half of the cake. Pour the chocolate glaze over the top of the cake and spread using a palette knife. If you wish you can decorate the cake using some fruit or seasonal decorations. I use little eggs and chickens at Easter time and have on occasion decorated this cake with a farm set!

**cake**
5 free range eggs — medium size
100g/4oz plain flour
25g/1oz cocoa powder
125g / 5oz caster sugar

**chocolate glaze**
75g/3oz dark chocolate
60g/2½oz butter, cut into cubes

**filling**
250ml cream /½ pint cream
Fruit of choice. In the summer I use strawberries or raspberries and in the winter I use tinned apricots or black cherries

# gingernut biscuits

**Divine on their own or served with grilled peaches and rhubarb fool.**

8oz/200g caster sugar
4oz/100g butter
1 tablespoon golden syrup
8oz/200g flour
2 teaspoons cinnamon
1 teaspoon ginger
1 teaspoon bicarbonate soda
1 egg

Preheat the oven to 150°C. Mix all ingredients together in a food processor until smooth a dough is formed. Break the dough into walnut size pieces and roll into balls. Place on a baking tray lined with baking parchment and flatten gently with two fingers. The biscuits spread quite a bit during cooking so allow for this when placing them on the tray. Bake for 23–30 minutes until dark brown. Remove from oven, leave on baking tray for five minutes so that the biscuits can set, then transfer to wire tray to cool.

# lemon drizzle cake

**lemon cake**
9oz/225g softened butter
9oz/225g caster sugar
zest and juice of 2 lemons
4 medium eggs
8oz/200g self-raising flour
1 tsp baking powder

**topping**
zest and juice of 1 lemon
4oz/100g caster sugar

**serves 6-8**

Heat the oven to 180°C. Butter an 8 inch/20cm round cake tin and line the base with parchment paper. Beat the butter and caster sugar in a large bowl until pale and creamy. Add the lemon zest and mix well. Whisk the eggs gradually into the butter mixture, beating well between each addition. Sift together the flour and baking powder and fold into the cake mixture using a large metal spoon. Add the lemon juice and fold until thoroughly combined. Spoon into the prepared cake tin and bake for 1 hour 15 minutes. Leave to cool in the tin. For the topping mix together the lemon juice, zest and sugar and then drizzle over the top of the cake while still warm.

gingernut biscuits, recipe opposite page

stanley christmas cake, recipe opposite page

# stanley christmas cake

This is a deliciously rich traditional Christmas cake recipe and the Stanley's even heat ensures that it is mouth-wateringly moist.

Line a 10 inch/25cm round cake tin or a deep 9 inch/23 cm square, with greaseproof paper. Heat oven to 140°C. Weigh the currants, sultanas, raisins, cherries and mixed peel into a bowl and pour over the whiskey and soak overnight. Sieve together the flour, mixed spice and ground nutmeg. Place all the ingredients in a large bowl and beat together using a wooden spoon until well mixed (about 5 minutes). Place the mixture into the prepared tin and smooth the top with a wet tablespoon. Bake in the pre heated Stanley for 5–6 hours. Check at intervals after 3 hours, as ovens tend to vary slightly. Cover the cake with double greaseproof paper for the last 1–2 hours, to prevent the cake from becoming too brown on top. Test the cake carefully using a skewer before removing (when the skewer comes out clean the cake is fully cooked). Leave the cake to cool in the tin overnight, turn out and remove the papers, and then wrap when completely cold in double greaseproof paper, then in foil and store in a cool dry place.

12oz/350g butter at room temperature
12oz/350g dark brown sugar
1lb/450g currants
12oz/350g sultanas
12oz/350g raisins
5oz/150g glacé cherries, halved
5oz/150g mixed cut peel
5oz/150g chopped almonds
Grated rind of 2 lemons
Grated rind of 1 orange
15oz/425g plain flour
1½ level teaspoons mixed spice
½ level teaspoon ground nutmeg
3oz/75g ground almonds
7 medium size free range eggs
3 tablespoons of whiskey

# children's favourites

## raspberry muffins

This is the perfect muffin recipe! The maize meal gives these muffins a nutty texture. This recipe uses raspberries but all berries can be used (including frozen berries). Add the berries to the muffin mixture when the mixture is in the muffin cases and push the berries down with your fingers. If you want to be especially wicked you can push a few white chocolate buttons into the muffin mixture – this works well with the raspberries.

Pre heat the oven to 200°C. Sieve the flour, baking powder and salt in to a bowl. Stir in the maize meal and castor sugar until mixed evenly. Beat the milk, eggs and oil and stir into the dry mixture. Divide the mixture evenly between the muffin cases, filling until about ¾ full. Add berries. Bake in a preheated oven until edges start to shrink away from the sides, approximately 20/25 minutes. Allow to cool for a few minutes before turning out onto a cooling tray. Serve warm. Allow 3 or 4 berries per muffin, about 5oz/150g. When using strawberries cut them in half.

10oz / 300g plain flour
1 tablespoon baking powder
¼ teaspoon salt
6oz/175g maize meal
5oz/150g castor sugar
4 free range eggs
12fl oz/350ml milk
6fl oz/175ml sunflower oil
½ teaspoon vanilla essence

**makes 12**

*The secret of muffins is to mix the dry ingredients in one bowl and the wet ingredients in another bowl, then add the wet to the dry. Do not over mix and don't worry if they look a bit lumpy. If the mixture is over mixed the result will be rubbery muffins.*

# wholemeal carrot and sultana muffins

Children love these for their "small break" at school where they make a healthy snack. These taste even better when made the night before and they freeze well.

Preheat the oven to 200°C. Sift both the flours and the baking powder into a mixing bowl. Add the sugar, grated carrots, sultanas, orange zest and salt, mix well. In another bowl mix the egg, sunflower oil and milk. Gently stir the wet ingredients into the dry ingredients. Spoon the mixture into the muffin cases and cook for about 15–20 minutes. Cool for 5 minutes and place on a wire rack.

6oz/150g plain flour
2oz/50g wholemeal flour
2 teaspoons of baking powder
Finely grated zest of 1 orange
4oz/100g grated carrot
4oz/100g sultanas
4oz/100g soft brown sugar
1 large free range egg
2 tablespoon sunflower oil
½ pint/ 275ml milk
¼ teaspoon salt

**makes 12 muffins**

# colourful queen cakes

I get enormous satisfaction from making and decorating these little buns. Let your imagination run wild when decorating them, children love to help!

Pre heat the oven to 180°C. Line two muffin tins with 24 muffin cases. Put butter, lemon zest, sugar, eggs, almonds and flour into a food processor and blend until evenly combined. Half fill each muffin case with a rounded tablespoon of cake mixture. Bake for 20 minutes until the cakes are golden, firm and risen. Leave to cool in the tins. Sift the icing sugar into a bowl, add 2 tablespoons of hot water, then stir until smooth. Divide two thirds of the icing between two further bowls. Dip a cocktail stick in the red colour, then stir into one bowl of icing until evenly coloured pink. Repeat with blue colouring in the second bowl of icing, then combine a drop of red and a drop of blue to make lilac in the third bowl. Stir well. Spoon icing sugar on to each cupcake. Decorate with your choice of sweeties, adding them before the icing sets. Leave to set for 20 minutes. Store in airtight container for up to two days.

**cakes**
4oz/125g unsalted butter,
softened and chopped
Finely grated zest of half a
lemon –
7oz/200g golden castor sugar
4 medium free range eggs
6oz/175g ground almonds
5oz/150g self raising flour

**icing**
3½oz/100g white icing sugar
Blue and red food colouring
24 or more jelly tots, jelly
babies, little eggs, silver balls or
hundred and thousands

**makes 24 cakes**

colourful queen cakes, recipe opposite page

desserts

lemon posset, recipe page 111

hot chocolate pudding, recipe page 110

# bramley apple and sultana crème brûlée

A seasonal twist to this classic dessert.

Put the apples, 2 tablespoons of lemon juice and 4 tablespoons of water in a saucepan. Cover and simmer over a gentle heat, for 15–20 minutes until the apples have pulped. Stir in the sultanas and set aside. Preheat the oven to 150°C. In a medium saucepan bring the cream and the cinnamon stick to a simmer over a moderate heat. Simmer for gently for 10 minutes. In a medium bowl whisk the egg yolks and sugar, gradually adding in the cream. Divide the apple and sultana mixture between the ramekins. Place the ramekins on a deep roasting tray, and place the tray in the oven. Carefully ladle or pour the cream mixture into the ramekins. Pour enough hot water into the roasting tray to come 2 inch up the sides of the ramekins. Bake for 20–30 minutes until the custard is set. Carefully remove the ramekins from the water bath and cool completely. Before serving, preheat grill to hottest setting and cover the surface of each custard with caster sugar. Put the ramekins under the hot grill for 1–2 minutes until the sugar has caramelised.

### Tip
I prefer to glaze the crème brûlée with a hand held gas torch, available for relatively little cost at hardware stores. Wave the ignited flame about 2 inches above each sugar dusted custard and let the flame melt the sugar, which will only take a couple of seconds.

**serves 8 x 6oz / 150ml**
**ovenproof ramekins**

# grilled peaches with amaretto

Grilling peaches is a sure sign that summer's here. This is a lovely easy dessert that looks fantastic.

Preheat the oven to 190°C. Preheat grill. Slice the peaches in half and remove stones. Place peach halves, cut side down and grill until each peach half has become slightly charred. Thinly slice the vanilla pod lengthways and scrape out seeds, mix seeds with castor sugar. Place the peach halves face up in a shallow ovenproof baking dish. Sprinkle the vanilla sugar over the peaches and pour in some of the amaretto. Place in the preheated oven and bake for 10 minutes. Pour over remaining amaretto and serve hot or cold with crème fraîche.

**serves 6**

# hot chocolate pudding

This is a foolproof recipe and should banish people's fears about making hot puddings!

Preheat the oven to 200°C. Grease eight ramekins. Dust with sugar. In a heavy saucepan, combine chocolate, butter, and cream; heat over low heat, stirring occasionally, until butter and chocolate melt and the mixture is smooth. Remove from heat. Add vanilla with a wire whisk, then stir in flour until the mixture is smooth. In a medium bowl with the mixer at high speed, beat sugar, eggs, and yolks until thick and lemon coloured — about 10 minutes. Fold the egg mixture into the chocolate, one-third at a time until fully blended. Divide batter evenly among prepared ramekins. Place cups in oven tray, bake until the edge of cake is set but the centre still jiggles — 8–9 minutes. Remove from oven, allow to cool for 3 minutes. Run a knife around the edge of the ramekin to loosen and invert onto dessert plates, serve immediately with whipped cream or vanilla ice-cream.

4oz/100g semisweet chocolate, chopped
4oz/100g butter/margarine cut into pieces
2½oz/60ml of heavy or whipping cream
½ teaspoon of vanilla extract
2oz/50g of all purpose flour
2oz/50g sugar
2 large eggs
2 large egg yolks
Whipped cream or vanilla ice-cream (optional)

**serves 8**

# panna cotta with winter fruit compôte

This traditional Italian dessert can be used in the wintertime with stewed dried fruits or in the summertime with stewed rhubarb and strawberries in rosewater (see page 17).

Put 450ml/¾ pint of the cream in a heavy-based pan with the seeds from the vanilla pod, lemon zest and sugar. Slowly bring to the boil, then strain into a bowl. Put the liqueur in a small heatproof bowl, sprinkle on the gelatin and leave until spongy, then stand the bowl over a pan of simmering water until the gelatin is dissolved. Stir a little of the cream into the gelatin mixture, then stir back into the rest of the cream; leave to cool. Whip the remaining cream in a bowl until soft peaks form and fold into the cooled cream. Pour into a serving bowl and chill for several hours until just set.

### Fruit compôte
Bring the sugar and water to the boil. Add the fruit, cinnamon and orange and simmer over a low heat for about 20 minutes until the fruit has swelled and liquid reduced substantially. Throw in the teabag. Remove after three minutes. Stir in the whiskey. Cool and refrigerate. Before serving the panna cotta, pour the winter fruit compote over the top. Cool in pan on wire rack (3 minutes). Run thin knife around cakes to loosen from sides of cups; invert onto dessert plates. Serve immediately with whipped cream or ice-cream.

**panna cotta**
600ml/1 pint double cream
1 vanilla pod, split and seeds extracted
grated zest of 1 lemon
2oz/50g caster sugar
2 teaspoons powdered gelatin
2 teaspoons amaretto di Saronno liqueur

**winter fruit compôte**
1 teabag
150g/5oz caster sugar
450ml/16fl oz water
1 cinnamon stick
peel of half orange
as much whiskey as you like
2 handfuls mixed dried fruits, such as cranberries, sultanas, apricots, figs, pears, stoned prunes

**serves 6 – 8**

# lemon posset

This dessert dates back to Victorian times. It must be the easiest dessert in the world!

Bring sugar and cream to the boil. Add lemon juice and whisk. Pour into six glasses and leave to set for 4 hours. Serve with a dollop of fresh cream and some shortbread biscuits.

**Tip**
If doubling the recipe, only increase the lemons to five, as it becomes too bitter.

1½ pints/450ml fresh cream
9oz/250g castor sugar
Juice of 3 organic lemons

**serves 6**

# passion fruit, mango and amaretto roulade

The Stanley is ideal for cooking meringue and meringue roulades achieving a sticky soft centre and a crisp finish.

Preheat the oven to 180°C. Beat the eggs and sugar together in a spotlessly clean bowl until meringue mixture holds a stiff peak. Line a swiss roll tin with tinfoil and brush with light oil. Spread the meringue gently over the tin with a palette knife. Bake in the pre heated oven for 15–20 minutes. Put a sheet of tinfoil on the work surface and the turn the roulade onto it. Remove the base tinfoil and allow to cool.

Peel the mango and chop flesh in food processor. Put in a bowl and add passion fruit seeds and juice. Add some sugar to taste. Cover and chill. Whip cream to soft peak stage, stir in crème fraîche and crushed amaretto biscuits. To assemble, turn the roulade out onto a sheet of parchment paper. Spread the cream mixture on the roulade, cover with a layer of fruit and roll the roulade up like a swiss roll.

**for the roulade**
6 egg whites
13oz/325g icing sugar

**for the filling**
600ml/1 pint cream
1 mango
2 passion fruit
Handful of amaretto biscuits crushed
1 tablespoon crème fraîche (optional)

**serves 6**

# rhubarb crumble

If you have any space at all in your garden, try growing some rhubarb. The early little pink stems are lovely and tender and give a pretty pink hue to the cooking syrup.

Preheat oven to 170°C. Sieve flour into a bowl; then rub in the chilled butter until the mixture resembles breadcrumbs. Add the oatflakes and half the sugar. Arrange half of the prepared fruit in an oven proof dish, sprinkle with the remaining sugar and top with remaining fruit. Spoon the crumble mixture over the fruit and cook until the fruit is soft and the topping golden. This will take approximately 25–30 minutes.

85g plain flour
25g butter chilled
110g sugar
55g oatflakes
450g rhubarb trimmed and cut into chunks

**serves 6**

# sticky toffee pudding served with butterscotch sauce

**Recipe by Gert Maes, Gaby's Restaurant, Killarney.**

### sticky toffee pudding
16 oz butter
6 oz self-raising flour
3 oz ground almonds
3 oz chopped almonds
6 oz brown sugar
4 beaten eggs
1 teaspoon vanilla essence

Cream the butter and sugar until the mixture turns a pale shade. Slowly add in the beaten eggs and vanilla essence. Sieve the ground almonds and flour together and fold into mixture. Lastly sprinkle in the finely chopped almonds. Bake at 160°C for 30 minutes. When baked, turn out and serve with plenty of butterscotch sauce.

### butterscotch sauce
16g butter
16g white sugar
16g brown sugar
2½ pints cream
½ juice of lemon

Melt the butter, white and brown sugars together until the mixture reaches the caramel stage. It should look like a soft light brown sticky mix. This should take approximately 10 minutes. Add the cream and bring the mixture to the boil, stirring well. Pass through a sieve and then stir in the lemon juice before serving.

**serves 6**

# chocolate pavlova

**The addition of chocolate makes this a truly spectacular looking dessert. Try to source organic cocoa powder (Green & Black is particularly good). To make a plain pavlova, substitute the cocoa powder with castor sugar.**

### pavlova
6 free range egg whites
11oz/275g icing sugar or
Caster sugar (I prefer to use icing sugar as I find it gives a nicer finish)
A pinch of salt
1 oz/25g cocoa powder silted

### filling
600ml /1 pint cream
4oz dark chocolate
an extra 4 tablespoons cream

Line two baking sheets with parchment paper and draw a 8 inch/22cm circle on each one. Preheat your Stanley oven to 150°C. Beat the egg whites, icing sugar and a pinch of salt with an electric whisk at full speed until the mixture forms stiff dry peaks. Fold in the cocoa powder. Divide the mixture between the two baking sheets and spread evenly using a palette knife making two circular shapes. Bake immediately for 45–55 minutes until the outside is crisp. Remove from oven and slide meringues still on the parchment paper onto a wire cooling tray. When the meringues are completely cooled carefully peel off the baking parchment. Whip the cream until it holds its shape. Sandwich the meringues together with half the whipped cream. Spoon the remainder of the whipped cream on top of the meringue sandwich. Melt the chocolate with the 4 tablespoons cream, stirring until the chocolate has melted. Allow to cool, then finish the meringue with a swirl of the chocolate sauce. Chill for a couple of hours before serving, this will allow the cream and meringue to amalgamate.

**serves 6 - 8**

rhubarb crumble, recipe page 111

stocks, sauces and relishes

A good, fresh flavoursome stock is the foundation for all soup recipes. The quality of the stock will more often than not dictate the richness and flavour of the soup. Make lots and store them in your freezer until needed.

## chicken stock

1 chicken carcass
2 medium onions peeled and quartered
2 medium carrots quartered
1 medium leek washed and sliced
4 sticks of celery halved
6 peppercorns
1 bayleaf
Handful of parsley with stalks
2 pints/1 litre of water

**makes approximately 1½ pints/900ml of stock**

Place all ingredients in a stockpot, add cold water and bring to the boil. Skim off any scum and move the pot to the coolest part of the hot plate and simmer for 3 hours. Skim and strain. Allow to cool, then chill in the fridge. When stock is chilled skim any fat off the stock with a metal spoon. Stock will hold in your fridge for 1 day, or you can freeze it.

## vegetable stock

3 onions chopped
5 medium carrots
3 medium leeks sliced
5 sticks of celery
A handful of parsley with stalks
3 sprigs of fresh thyme
1 bayleaf
6 peppercorns
A pinch of salt
6 pints/ 3½ litres of cold water

**makes 4½ pints /2½ litres**

Place all ingredients in a stockpot, add cold water and bring to the boil. Skim off any scum and move the pot to the coolest part of the hot plate and simmer for 1 hour. Skim and strain. Allow to cool, then chill in the fridge.

## beef stock

3lbs beef bones (ask your butcher for marrow bones)
7 pints/3½ litres of water
2 onions halved
2 medium carrots halved
2 medium leeks halved
A few fresh sprigs of parsley stalks
2 bay leaves
6 black peppercorns
A pinch of salt

**makes 42 pints /22 litres**

Place all ingredients in a stockpot, add cold water and bring to the boil. Skim off any scum and move the pot to the coolest part of the hot plate and simmer for 1 hour. Skim and strain. Allow to cool, then chill in the fridge.

## fish stock

Sweat the vegetables in the butter over a moderate heat until they are soft but not coloured. Add the fish bones and cook for a further 1 minute. Add the cold water and wine and bring back to the boil. Skim off any impurities. Add the lemon slices, herbs and black peppercorns and simmer for a further 20 minutes. Pass through a sieve.

**makes approximately
3 pints/1800ml**

## mayonnaise

Place all ingredients except the olive oil into a food processor and blend until creamy. With the blade motor still running, pour in the oil through the feeder tube, in a steady stream, until the mayonnaise is thick. Thin if necessary with a little hot water. Store in a covered container in a fridge for up to 3 days.

## pickled cucumber

Slice the cucumber as thinly as you can. Salt, rest and rinse the cucumber. While the cucumber is resting, bring the sugar and vinegar to the boil and reduce for 30 seconds. Take off the heat and allow to cool completely. Dry the cucumbers, place in a bowl and add the liquid. This will keep in the fridge for 2 –3 days.

## tomato sauce basic recipe

The tomato sauce recipe given below is tasty and versatile. I make this sauce in huge quantities and freeze it in small amounts. We use it as a sauce on grilled chicken, fish, with pasta and on pizzas, in fact it crops up all over the place.

Gently fry onion and garlic in olive oil, for five minutes. Do not let the onion and garlic colour. Add chopped tomatoes, tomato purée and sugar. Allow tomato mixture to simmer for 10 minutes.
Add basil. Blend sauce in liquidiser.

## redcurrant jelly

Wash and clean the redcurrants but do not remove the stems. Put into a heavy based saucepan and cook gently on the simmering plate for 30–40 minutes until the juice has run out and the currants are broken down. Strain the fruit through fine muslin, do not press the fruit as the jelly will be cloudy. Leave to drain overnight. Measure the juice and allow 14lb/625g of sugar to each pint/600ml of juice. Add the sugar to the juice and dissolve on the simmering plate, stirring carefully. Then boil rapidly on the hot plate for 2 minutes. This jelly starts to set in a few minutes and should be poured into hot jars immediately.

## pear chutney

Put all ingredients into a wide stainless steel pot and simmer over a moderate heat until soft and pulpy and slightly thickened — about 1½–2 hours. It will reduce to about a ⅓ of the original volume. Pot in sterilised jars and seal tightly. Allow to mature for 3–4 weeks before using.

**makes 6-8 x 1lb/450g Pots**

## blackberry jam

Put all the blackberries in to the preserving pan with the water and lemon juice and cook on the simmering plate until the fruit is soft and well broken down. This should take about 30 minutes.
Remove from the heat and add the sugar, stir until dissolved. Bring this to the boil and boil rapidly for 45 minutes until setting point is reached. Remove any scum from the surface. Fill the warm jars nearly to the rim and place a round of waxed paper on at once, excluding any pockets of air. Then cover and seal.

**makes 3½lbs /1.6kg**

## onion marmalade

Put the sliced onions into a large frying pan. Pour balsamic vinegar and olive oil over onions and add brown sugar. Bring the contents of the pan to the boil, then reduce heat and move frying pan over to the simmering plate and simmer gently, stirring occasionally until the onion mixture is thick and brown.
Allow to cool. This can be stored in a fridge for up to two weeks.

# cooking with your Stanley

# cooker operation

## Stanley cast iron range cookers

Because your Stanley is made from cast iron, it has wonderful cooking qualities. Heat distribution is radiated from all sides which ensures that food retains its moisture and the oven does not dry or shrink the food as it is cooked. Casseroles and roasts are particularly delicious in the Stanley as the gentle heat tenderises meat and seals in juices and flavours. The Stanley also allows you to cook foods that require different temperatures in the same oven. For example, you can slow-cook a casserole while crisping pizza and quiche bases on the floor of the oven. Oven cooking smells are vented outside, reducing condensation in the kitchen.

## The main oven

The main oven is for baking and roasting. Its large capacity (390 x 310 x 406mm) will hold a large turkey and allows you to cook for large groups comfortably. The door has an attractive thermostat feature which indicates whether the oven is hot or cold. There are two chromed steel shelves and four shelf positions for maximum cooking capacity.

The main oven is controlled by the oven thermostat which is calibrated to the centre of the oven. If you select a given temperature, the centre of the oven will reach this temperature while the top will be a shade hotter and the bottom will be slightly cooler, allowing you to cook foods that require different temperatures in the same oven. Don't worry about lifting the insulating lids on the hotplate, it won't affect the oven temperature.

Once the oven has heated up, its cast iron construction retains heat for quite some time and even after the oven has been switched off, it takes quite some time to cool down. It cools down at a rate of 20°C per minute at higher temperatures and 10°C per minute below 150°C. It can take up to four hours for a cooker to cool down completely. Dishes such as casseroles can work out very economically, because after a very short time you can turn off the cooker and allow the food to continue cooking slowly for several hours.

In terms of cookware, your traditional baking tins and trays will generally be fine. For casseroles and roasts, cookware with a steel base and an enamel coating is excellent and Stanley offers a range of bespoke cookware designed specifically for best results.

## The lower oven

The additional lower oven in the Brandon measures 390 x 220 x 406mm and has one chromed shelf with two shelf positions. It also has a cast iron interior and is marvellous for slow-cooking. The temperature of the lower oven is approximately half that of the main oven and once again, the top of this oven is hotter than the bottom.

The lower oven is enormously useful when you are cooking for a big group or having a baking session. For example, you can start your Sunday roast in the main oven and an hour before serving turn the temperature up for roast vegetables. You can then move the meat to the lower oven to finish cooking. Then when the main oven is switched off, there may still be enough heat to pop in a dessert!

It is important to remember that when baking, the side of the cooker closest to the burner will be slightly hotter, so you will need to turn it at least once or twice.

# The hotplate

One of the best features of the Stanley is the hotplate. Its large size means heat is distributed evenly to large pots and pans (perfect for risottos and tortillas!) and it is machine ground for maximum heat transfer to your cookware. Four average sized pots will fit on the main hotplate at any one time and a small one on the simmering plate.

The simmer plate is very useful for keeping vegetables, sauces or gravies on a gentle simmer while finishing off cooking your meal. For a continuous supply of hot water, just leave a kettle of water on the simmer plate.

The temperature of the hotplate is controlled by the oven thermostat. An oven thermostat setting of 200°C will normally give you the heat you require and if you need a hotter hotplate, simply turn the oven thermostat up to a higher setting.

The hottest part of the hotplate is in the centre over the oven burner and there is a gradient reduction in temperature to the right.

It is important to point out that the type of cookware you use will effect the hotplate's performance. Good contact between hotplate and pan is essential and a heavy based machine ground pot or pan should always be used. The Stanley range of cast iron cookware has been specifically designed to optimise range cooking performance, contact Waterford Stanley for more details on the range of cookware available.

# The Stanley Supreme

The Stanley Supreme combines the timeless qualities and unique styling of Stanley's traditional cast iron cookers with state of the features to suit modern lifestyles. Offering no less than five distinct cooking features, the Supreme gives you creative control, ease of use and total flexibility in the kitchen.

## The slow cooking oven

Slow cooking adds superb flavour to your food. The Supreme's slow oven is themostatically controlled with a low setting of between 110 and 120°C.

## Hob

Both the dual fuel and ceramic hobs in the Supreme offer five distinct cooking zones and feature a full-length fish burner.

## Advanced ceramic hob

With virtually instant response and an option to grill on full or 'centre-only' settings, the grill is also entirely separate from the main ovens.

## Fan ovens

At the heart of the Stanley Supreme are two independent, fully automatic fan ovens. For total precision, the left-hand oven is fully-programmable and thermostatically controlled.

# caring for your stanley

**A Stanley will be a showpiece in your home for many years to come! Care for it, and it will be a lifelong companion.**

The vitreous enamel finish on your Stanley is tough and hard wearing but should be treated with care. Clean the front, sides and hob by wiping it with a warm soapy cloth and then giving it a quick polish with a dry cloth. Do not use an abrasive cleaning material on the vitreous enamel.

Acidic spills on the hob should be wiped off immediately with a clean, dry cloth. If there are stubborn marks on the hob, use a good quality enamel cleaner. We recommend the use of Stanley enamel cleaners on all Stanley range cookers. The cleaners have been specially formulated to clean and maintain the enamel finish. For those models with stainless steel or chrome trim, we also have a stainless steel cleaner.

The hotplate on cast iron ranges will carbonise any food spilt on it and any such spills should be removed with a wire brush or metal scraper; it is important to do this to ensure good contact between your cookware and the hotplate. Take care when cleaning the insulating lids as the hotplate may be hot.

# commissioning and servicing

To achieve optimum performance your Stanley cast iron range cooker must be commissioned by an authorised Stanley service agent. We recommend that cookers are serviced every 12 months. All gas appliances should be checked regularly by a service engineer. Please contact Waterford Stanley for a list of authorised agents who have been trained by our technical team on our range cookers.

# index

# enjoy!

You have come to the end of the cookbook, but we hope that this marks the start of many happy years of cooking on your Stanley. Each Stanley range cooker has been designed for quality, durability and cooking performance. The first Stanley was manufactured in 1934 and since then we have developed a reputation for the excellent build and wonderful cooking and heating qualities of our range cookers.

Our Stanley stoves perfectly complement the range cookers. Handcrafted from cast iron with superior efficiency and precision control these stoves bring a warm ambience to every home and are available in a variety of fuel options.

For those seeking cooking and heating solutions with a more contemporary style, look to the Waterford Appliances collection. This collection offers a tailormade solution for every lifestyle achieving an elegant balance between build quality, performance and a design style that endures. The collection includes range cookers, built-in ovens and hobs, extractor hoods and refrigeration products. See the entire collection at **www.waterford-appliances.com**

For more details on our full product range please visit our website on **www.waterfordstanley.com** or call Waterford Stanley Ltd. on **lo-call 1850 302502** for your nearest stockist.

### Stanley Ranges

Traditional cast-iron range cookers available in oil, solid fuel and natural gas models, capable of heating up to 20 radiators.

### Stanley Supreme

Uniting the timeless quality and unique styling of Stanley with modern functionality, the Supreme can be fitted directly into your kitchen without flues or fuss.

### Waterford Appliances

Contemporary collection of appliances that conform to Aga premium quality and high build standards while delivering excellent value for money.

### Stanley Stoves

Traditional cast-iron stoves available in electric, solid fuel, natural gas and oil, boiler and non-boiler models.